"How I Learned
to Speak Dog"

& Other Animal Stories

To Ann,

Merry Christmas 1995

With Love,

Dawn + Wayne

xoxo

"How I Learned to Speak Dog"

& Other Animal Stories

Collected by the British Columbia S.P.C.A.

Foreword by Vicki Gabereau

Douglas & McIntyre
Vancouver / Toronto

Douglas & McIntyre
1615 Venables Street
Vancouver, British Columbia
V5L 2H1

Canadian Cataloguing in Publication Data

Main entry under title:
How I learned to speak dog and other animal stories

ISBN 1-55054-427-6

1. Animals — Anecdotes.   I. British Columbia Society for the Prevention of Cruelty to Animals.
QL791.H68 1995   636   C95-910546-8

Editing by Barbara Pulling
Cover illustration by Rose Cowles
Cover and text design by Rose Cowles
Typeset by Brenda and Neil West, BN Typographics West
Printed and bound in Canada by Best Gagné Book Manufacturers Ltd.
Printed on acid-free paper ∞

The publisher gratefully acknowledges the assistance of the Canada Council and of the British Columbia Ministry of Tourism, Small Business and Culture for its publishing programs.

The following work was previously published and appears here with permission: "Lum King's Horse" by Norma Charles from *Coquitlam — 100 Years* (District of Coquitlam); "Pig" from *The Collected Poems* by Leona Gom (Sono Nis Press, 1991); "Avalanche and the Chicken Lady" by Deanna Kawatski from *Wilderness Mother* (Whitecap Books, 1994); "Whale Watching" by Sandy Shreve from *Bewildered Rituals* (Polestar Press Ltd., 1011 Commercial Drive, Vancouver, B.C., Canada V5L 3X1); "The Souls of Animals" by Lorna Crozier from *Everything Arrives at the Light* (McClelland & Stewart, 1995).

CONTENTS

II. Country Living

III. In From the Wild

Foreword
Vicki Gabereau

The care, feeding and general adoring of animals has long been one of my favourite pastimes. So naturally the S.P.C.A. is one of my favourite causes. I am delighted to be introducing to you this entertaining collection of animal stories published to celebrate the B.C. S.P.C.A.'s 100th anniversary. And I just can't resist the opportunity to tell you a short animal story of my own.

It is possible that I am forgetting one, but my calculations indicate ownership over the past forty years of the following animals: six cats, six dogs, one turtle, two gerbils and an assortment of fish, all handsomely named and uniformly doted upon. Some were rescued, some came from shelters and several just walked in the door and never left. Only one was purchased, found sitting in a pet store window looking for all the world like a cartoon puppy. Hilda the bull terrier was three months old when I got her, and she could eat through cement. She was a dog possessed of an odd personality and would bend to the will of almost no one. She was a trial, but she was awfully fond of me. She was, however, not fond of my friend Elliott the lawyer, whom she chased around the living room until he climbed up the bookcase. (Not a bad place for him, come to think of it.) After being appropriately chastised, she promised me she'd never do that again.

But Hilda saved me from a robber one night. I had gone to check on a noise in the backyard. Undeterred by my appearance in the doorway, a man dressed in dark clothing continued to vault over the fence. Apparently I was not seen as a menace by this professional. But he had a different reaction to my dog. I should point out here that Hilda and I were velcroed together — I could rarely make a move without her. Even though it drove me a bit mad, on this night I was grateful. She arrived at my side as Mr. Robber steamed towards me. The steam evaporated when he caught sight of my little pig dog and she of him. He froze as Hilda began to make a particularly alarming sound: not a bark, not a growl, but a sort of sucking noise. Primeval, really. It was truly scary. As if he were in a film that was being rewound, the guy retreated. I was proud of Hilda. She'd done something useful and she knew it. I gave her a cookie and called the cops. Hilda mellowed slightly after our episode — but only slightly.

I hope this small tale has whetted your appetite for what is to follow. Enjoy the book. Support the S.P.C.A. And for heaven's sake keep loving those animals.

Introduction

Human attitudes towards other species are shifting these days, moving from a predominantly exploitative model to one that is more humane and ecological. This shift has been progressively more pronounced among young people for several decades — a trend that bodes well for all creatures, including humans. So much of our nature as individuals, as a culture and as a species is revealed in our relationships with animals.

This year the B.C. Society for the Prevention of Cruelty to Animals celebrates its 100th anniversary, and our centennial provides us with an ideal occasion to present some of British Columbians' most memorable animal encounters. Selected from hundreds of submissions, the stories and poems in this book will make you laugh, make you cry and make you wonder. They come from all parts of the province and feature all kinds of animals: dogs, cats, horses, rabbits, squirrels, grizzly bears, wolves, whales, a beaver, a moose — and even a boa constrictor! These stories are about personal relationships. The reader may notice that there are no stories about intensive farming, animals in research or fur trapping — practices that make up a significant part of the human-animal economy. Their absence here should not be taken as an indication that the S.P.C.A. is not concerned with the welfare of all animals. Indeed, the society has committees working for improvements in each of these areas.

Education plays a crucial role in the S.P.C.A.'s efforts to prevent cruelty to animals. All royalties from the sale of *How I Learned to Speak Dog and Other Animal Stories* will be directed to the classroom and community humane education programs of the B.C. S.P.C.A.'s educational affiliate, the B.C. Humane Education Society, and its partner agency in this project, the Northwest Wildlife Preservation Society. By teaching children about the behaviour, needs and care of animals, humane education provides gentle yet powerful lessons in compassion, responsibility and respect for others.

We hope that these stories will amuse, amaze and move you. They may even change your view of animals...

Stephen Huddart
Executive Director
B.C. Humane Education Society

I: Domestic Bliss?

Lesson of Love

Michele Carter

My pup Jazz, a white standard poodle, was ready for obedience class. He had spent nine months frolicking with his pals through wooded trails, fetching sticks and balls, rolling in mud, crouching in wet leaves and generally enjoying a pup's life. Overall, he was a good dog, except for one particularly annoying habit: he loved to eat tissues and plastic sandwich bags.

Try as I would, I could not get him to come once he had snapped up one of these delicacies. Instead, he would dangle the thing from his mouth, taunt me from a distance out of arm's reach, and then, as I lunged for the last shred of stuff hanging from his tooth, suck it back, *phoop*, with the efficiency of a Hoover. He loved this game; I hated it. No matter what I did, I couldn't catch him, because he would not come when I called. Jazz had to learn the recall — to come to me no matter what. Obedience classes were always at the back of my mind, but not until "the incident" did I emphatically decide to sign up.

The incident occurred on a sunny day in May. Jazz had popped in to visit his friend Rubio, a white Afghan with a fenced backyard. We had just stepped onto the grass when Jazz spied a tasty morsel lying next to the lawn chair. I, too, saw the object but mistakenly reasoned that it was too big to swallow. Also, not being plastic or paper, it didn't fall into the category of a Jazzy edible. I was wrong on both counts.

To the lay person, the object was harmless, but to the connoisseur? A must-have, especially since Rubio might want it too. What was the tempting treat? A man's brown suede garden glove.

Jazz raced over and captured it. I screamed to my friend to tackle him, but the man thought I was kidding. As I laboured to catch Jazz, I called out for help, but the man went into the house for refreshments. Jazz skipped and pranced in front of me, gaily swinging the glove as he romped across the yard. Pausing briefly, he turned towards me; he stopped. I spoke to him, pleaded with him to give me the glove. With outstretched hand I ventured closer. I almost had him. I lunged; he turned and bolted. I collapsed on the grass. When I raised my head, Jazz was a few feet away, artfully manoeuvring each finger into his mouth. I knew it was hopeless, but I attacked once more as the entire glove disappeared behind closed lips. As the man brought out our lemonade, Jazz gulped down the glove, expelling a slight cough as it scratched his throat. The incident took approximately two minutes.

Two hours later, Jazz was on the operating table. The vet told me that dogs don't pass suede garden gloves, nor do they pass pantyhose or tennis balls, other items that he had found in dogs' stomachs. With the help of video endoscopy, the vet was able to fish out the glove and pull it up through Jazz's throat without having to cut him open.

"You'd be surprised how elastic the throat is," he said. "But don't count on them being able to get rid of these things on their own. The dog gets dehydrated and within two days could be dead. It's best to get them in here for treatment as soon as possible."

Nine hundred dollars later, Jazz was enrolled in obedience class.

Jazz's beginner's class was held in a church basement. They must have chosen the place for its extraordinary acoustics: the barking and yelping echoed so powerfully off the walls, it sounded as if there were three hundred dogs taking their first class, not just fifteen.

Out of those fifteen *big* dogs were fourteen males. Male dogs believe their role in life is to dominate all creatures great and not so great, so the first hour was spent wrestling our dogs to the ground to keep them from tearing each other's hearts out. "Perfectly normal," the instructor had screamed encouragingly.

"What did he say?" I yelled to the woman next to me with the German shepherd. "He said don't be so formal," she yelled back in reply. After that we all wore sweatshirts and jeans.

The dogs were to complete a rigorous eight-week program to become well-behaved and socialized pets, so that when they disrupted the social order by, say, eating an entire container of frozen soup left in the sink to thaw for dinner, they would know enough to look pathetic and exhibit remorse.

With the constant cacophony of dogs expressing their excitement, we never heard a word the instructor said. We simply watched and imitated his actions. The class was more theatre of the absurd than dramatic realism, but we persevered because we wanted our companion animals to be well-mannered canine citizens.

Obedience classes, by the way, are not just for dogs. A companion human must be in attendance at all times. We learn to bend, pat and coo "gooboyee" when the dog does well and to shout "No!" when he does *not* do so well, like when he snarls at a neighbour dog for encroaching a paw or tail onto his smidgen of territory on the socialization mat. Companion humans march around the hall giving quick snaps to the chokers and saying "heel." We speak deeply and command our dogs to "stay." We step on their leashes to help them learn "down." In most cases, the dogs already knew the sit command, except for Bobo, the black lab.

Bobo was not doing so well in the class. Undaunted, she maintained an expression of determined good will, happy to be invited to the room. Always smiling, Bobo wriggled and squirmed, darting her head this way and that, looking for someone to play with. When she spotted a likely pal, she yanked on her leash and barked at her human, "C'mon, over here." Then, like a drunken frog, she leaped in the opposite direction and barked, "No, no, I meant over here."

At a year and a half, Bobo still could not grasp the dynamics of the sit command. She knew you wanted her bottom to scrunch up to her hind legs, and she knew it meant a lot to you, but the best she could do was hover above the ground, wagging her tail at breakneck speed like a pendulum gone awry.

Once, the instructor knocked on Bobo's skull and announced to the class, "Ah, that explains it. No brain. This unfortunate beast was born with just a brainstem." Bobo's classmates, audibly impressed with her distinct stature in the group, growled a low "cool" and panted their approval.

Obedience class would not be complete, though, without the class goof. Being a goof is different from being a brainstem. A goof cracks up the other dogs with his crazy antics, making them snicker and snort with glee. Lucky, the golden retriever, was our class goof.

Lucky's down-stays turned into luxurious back rubs in which he waved all four legs in the air, indiscriminately batting and bashing the dogs on either side of him. He deserved a gold star in goofiness for shaking his head so hard that yellow guck flew out and for being faster than his human in the race to get to it — to eat it, in Lucky's case.

But in the last week, Lucky earned himself the Grand Prize for Goofiness. As his human was trying to get him to sit, Lucky was sure he saw a squirrel dart underneath his tail. He whipped around so fast that his head slipped out of his collar. Not giving the squirrel a second thought, he bounded into the middle of the room, declaring, "I'm free! I'm free!"

His floppy paws were slip-sliding all over the place, up and down the floor like a golden-haired Gretzky. He was jumping and spinning so fast his companion human couldn't catch him. The dogs were barking and hacking, straining at their leashes to get a better look. Lucky's human tried to grab his neck and put the collar back on, but the dog was too bouncy, too quick, too goofy.

Suddenly, the instructor raced over to his black bag in the corner. The dogs howled the alarm to Lucky. Lucky poised himself for the worst, but he wasn't ready for this.

He saw the instructor pull what appeared to be a slimy octopus from the black bag. Before Lucky could run home, the slippery sea creature was on his back and around his neck. He shrank in fear and, in his final act of goofiness, peed a great huge puddle right there at the instructor's feet. The dogs went wild, barking and yowling, jumping in place, pawing the floor in delirium. Lucky slunk back in line with the instructor's leash wrapped around him and his "class goof" title intact.

At the end of the eight weeks, eleven dogs, including Jazz, graduated to advanced beginners. After plenty of coaxing and practice, he has learned to come when he's called. Now if he has something in his mouth and I tell him to drop it, he does.

We humans learned something, too. We learned that with a big bowl of patience and love we can teach our dogs important life skills. With practice, they inevitably learn because they love their companion humans and want to please them. No matter where we come from or where we're heading, we all want the best for our dogs.

We companion humans share another common bond: we love our dogs, be they Hoover, Brainstem or Goof.

Who Was Cleo?
Vidyut Aklujkar

I must admit, I am partial to cats. And the feeling is reciprocal. Cats adore me. When I go for a morning walk along the dike on River Road in Richmond, three or four tabbies come out to rub against me or walk beside me. One white aristocratic Persian sitting on the bonnet of his master's Volvo greets me regularly with a flicker of his left ear. One of my neighbours has a tomcat; as I settle down in his living room sipping tea, I can anticipate when the cat will bounce onto my lap, where I can send him to heights of purring ecstasy by gently stroking under his chin.

But even with all this experience with cats, I was not prepared for Cleo, who was named after Cleopatra, the Queen of the Nile. Perhaps the circumstances of our introduction had something to do with it. Some years ago I was the divisional supervisor for the Canadian Heart Fund in the Riverdale area, and was making a round of routine phone calls to enlist new volunteers. I dialled a number from the list in my area, and as I heard a female voice answer, I said, "Hello, I am calling on behalf of the Canadian Heart Fund. Is this Mrs. Jiwani?"

The reply I heard sounded something like, "Hey, get your tail out of my armpit."

I was taken aback. I mean, I do like cats. I don't deny that, in my childhood in India, I may have fancied myself turning into an alley cat and roaming around the streets of Bombay without heeding the evening curfew regulations so restrictive to girls from respectable families, but *this* was not on my imaginary palette. Besides, this Mrs. Jiwani whom I was calling for the first time in my life had no way of knowing my childhood fancies. Before I could stutter "I beg your pardon," the voice at the other end apologized profusely in English with a Gujarati lilt, and after determining the purpose of my phone call assured me that yes, indeed, she was more than willing to be a door-to-door canvasser for this worthy cause. With that welcome assurance I was willing to pardon her first rude reply, whatever its cause might have been. Within a short while our phone calls turned into visits, and casual visits gave way to a friendship that over the years has become as thick as the Indian tea we love to drink with lots of milk and sugar and aromatic cardamom.

Mrs. Jiwani, or as I call her now, Banoo, explained to me the source of that puzzling reply over the phone. Cleo was the one to blame. That warm afternoon, Banoo was sitting on the sofa, stitching a nightie for Munni, her daughter. Cleo was sitting beside her on the arm of the sofa, keeping an eye on Banoo's handiwork. As the phone rang, Banoo reached over Cleo to the side table to answer it. As she said "Hello," Cleo's raised tail tickled her bare armpit like a scouring brush, and Banoo blurted out that admonition to her dear old cat. After getting to know Cleo, I could very well imagine the scene, and it made me break into giggles.

Cleo was not like any other cat I had known. She was not at all like a cat. When I met her, she looked more like an old raccoon that had forgotten to wear his eye-patch. She was hugely overweight, and strange, too. Her body looked like an overfilled sack of ashes. The colour of her coat was steel grey. Her piercing eyes were very, very yellow. The combination resembled two stray buttercups in an overgrown patch of dusty miller. And there was always an accusation in those eyes.

The way Cleo meowed was enough to make you get up from whatever you were doing and wonder which house was on fire. She meowed like a siren. But with her voice and her personality she definitely ruled the entire neighbourhood. One day as we were sitting in Banoo's backyard around a sizzling barbecue, Cleo came out, having finished her nap, and demanded food in her usual complaining tone. Before Banoo got up, the neighbour's dog, which had been frolicking in his own backyard, took to his heels and, with his tail between his hind legs, ran inside and hid under his master's bed. We roared with laughter, but Cleo took it in stride. After all, she was Cleo, the queen of the territory, and it was her birthright to get due respect from the lowly canines of the neighbourhood.

Banoo gave Cleo the respect a good Indian housewife gives to her mother-in-law. Cleo would demand food in her shrill voice at four o'clock every morning. Banoo would nudge her husband to get up as if it were a call for the morning prayers from the mosque. He would get up to give Cleo what she wanted, but he often complained about it. Sometimes Cleo would sniff her dish and walk away with a wrinkled nose. Then Banoo would be under stress for days to detect the cause of Her Majesty's dislike and make amends for the oversight. I was puzzled over this hierarchy in the family but did not venture to ask. One day, after Banoo had decided that I was a cat person and that she could trust me with her guarded secrets, I heard the reason.

"Vidyut, do you know who Cleo really is? She is my African maid, Bwanabona," Banoo said in a voice full of awe and confidence. This did not make sense, let alone explain the reverent treatment given to the pet. But by this time I had grown familiar with Banoo's style of logic, so I waited patiently for more light on the subject. Banoo was given to sketching vivid scenarios of her own afterlife. One day, for example, all I had asked her was a simple question: "Whose sweater are you knitting?" To that, with grave seriousness, she had replied, "You know, Vidyut, all my life I have knitted everyone around me a sweater, a cardigan, a pullover, a bolero or a poncho. Ali has got half a dozen and all my children got a new one every year. But now I am getting old, and one day I will die and go up to Allah Mian's house. There Allah Mian will ask me, 'Banoo, I hear you have knitted everyone in the family a sweater.' I will have to say to Him, with truth and modesty, 'Yes, Allah Mian, I have.' He will then ask me, 'Well, in all those years, did you knit a sweater for yourself?' And if I say 'No, I forgot,' then He will say, 'You fool, I gave you a long life, how did you forget to make a sweater for yourself? Now go back and make one for yourself, before you die and come up here.' Then what will I do? I would hate to come back from up there just to finish making a sweater. So, I said to myself, 'Banoo, you better make a sweater for yourself,' and that's who this is for."

I had become accustomed to hearing about her own afterlife in Banoo's usual yarn-twisting style, but this was something new. Here she was telling me about her cat's former life. I pricked my ears to hear more. Banoo was serious. This is what she told me. Bwanabona was the maid of her husband's family in Uganda. She had been with them ever since their family migrated from India to Uganda. Banoo's husband, Ali, was a toddler then. Bwanabona had doted on him like a mother hen. When Ali married Banoo, Bwanabona had to put up with this young mistress. Bwanabona had set ideas about how a girl should eat well and make herself worthy of childbearing. But the young mistress was more like a tapered candlestick. She was picky with her food. No plump layers of flesh on her that Bwanabona could decorate to her heart's content. Besides, the young mistress's taste in clothes was rather subdued, like that of the British, not like Ali's mother's or like Bwanabona's own. Till then, Ali's mother had let Bwanabona be in charge of all her children. With Banoo, that was not to be. Banoo decided what her children were to eat, wear or play with. Bwanabona used to complain to Ali's mother. The old lady would humour her out of respect for her many years of service with the family.

"That should tell you why Cleo always gives me this accusing look. Bwanabona was more of a mother-in-law to me than Ali's mother, may she rest in peace. Bwanabona never trusted me with the well-being of my own family," Banoo concluded.

"This is too much, Banoo," I said. "I agree I have not seen that kind of look in any cat's eyes so far. But why your maid from Africa? Why would she become a cat in Canada?"

"You know why? Because if we had stayed in Uganda, then by now we would have supported her. We would have given her a pension for all her long years of loyal service. But that was not to be. The tyrant Idi Amin robbed everyone. He robbed us of our house and property that we had acquired with hard work, and he robbed his own people, like Bwanabona, of the rewards they would have reaped for their lifelong hard work. All those servants would be earning a good pension from their masters and living in peace in their ripe old age on our property. When we had to leave the country under duress, Bwanabona could not stop crying. She had raised all my mother-in-law's children, and all mine too. Never being able to see them again was too painful for her. But Bwanabona was clever. She had faith in magic. She came here and became a cat. You know how a year after we came to this house, Cleo came and adopted us out of nowhere."

"I still don't get the connection, Banoo. What makes you believe that this grouchy Canadian cat of yours is the same old African maid?"

"You want proof? Then hear this. You know how much I have to spend every month on Cleo's food? You convert that to our currency in Uganda. That is exactly the amount of pension that I would have to give to Bwanabona every month. That's not counting the vet's bills, of course. We would have paid all her medical bills in Uganda anyway."

This conclusive "proof," in Banoo's view, silenced me, although I can't say that it convinced me. But who was I to doubt Banoo's belief if it relieved her sense of justice and added to her joy?

Learning about Cleo's previous life certainly seemed to explain some queer habits of hers. She was not a cat who cared for milk, while all the cats I had known in India were ardent friends of the milkman. Peanut butter, bananas and chopped meat were Cleo's favourite foods. Those were definitely the telltale signs of her former life to Banoo. Cleo was the terror of the neighbourhood and even tamed irreverent dogs. However, she clearly defied the proverbial relationship between a cat and a mouse. In the old house of the Jiwani family, one day a mouse came scurrying onto their kitchen patio, obviously visiting from the large overgrown field nearby. Cleo took one look at the mouse, bolted in the other direction and climbed over the fence of their garden to be safely away from the little rodent. I happened to be sitting in Banoo's kitchen and so was an eyewitness to the scene, or else I would not have believed it. "Bwanabona would throw whatever she had in hand and jump over a table, if she ever saw a mouse," confirmed Banoo.

Cleo died last week at the ripe old age of eighteen. Bwanabona would have been eighty-two this year. Cleo died in Munni's lap. Munni is Banoo's youngest, her only daughter among the four Jiwani sons. It was fit that Cleo, a.k.a. Bwanabona, should die in Munni's lap, because this "end flower" on the branch of the Jiwani family tree, as she used to call Munni, was her favourite "grandchild" of her master's family. Banoo had once told me a story about Bwanabona's mulish stubbornness when it came to Munni's well-being.

"You know, Munni was five, and I had made for her a beautiful yellow dress. It had frills, and I had embroidered little flowers on the collar. She was very fond of that dress and would love to wear it to parties. One day, early morning, Bwanabona came rushing into my room and demanded that I give her the dress. When I did, she pleaded and pleaded with me never to let Munni wear that dress again. I did not understand why. She was very scared and tears were running down her cheeks. From her sobs and her wild handshakes and her agitated talk, what I gathered was this: she had had a nightmare and had seen Munni wearing that dress run and fall into a ditch and hurt herself. That was enough. She would not leave until I made her a promise, and then too, she did not let me rest until I took the dress and donated it to an orphanage in our city. That's how stubborn she was when it came to Munni."

So, this is what happened on Cleo's last Saturday. Munni, now married, had come from her own home in Clearbrook to her mother's in Richmond for a little visit, and had fed Cleo her favourite food. Cleo had become very old and had gone deaf. All day long she would mostly nestle into her basket and would not pay much attention to visitors at Banoo's house. But she got up as she saw Munni. After eating a little, she meowed in a thin voice, and Munni sat down to pet her. Cleo climbed up in her lap, curled up, looked into Munni's eyes and breathed her last. I grieved along with the Jiwanis, but Banoo's grief cloud had a silver lining. She had a sense of fulfilment, of having given shelter to a long-lost servant till her last day. They buried Cleo in the garden and planted a hydrangea bush on the site. Bwanabona used to wear a favourite dress with large purple hydrangeas all over, and she loved to be in the garden in all her spare time.

Birdy
Janice Johnson

I first made the acquaintance of Birdy in Coal Harbour, Vancouver. We were in the marine construction business and were fixing up an existing marina. It was a beautiful spring day and I was working on one of the floats. As I turned to pick up a wrench, I saw one of the other crew members walking towards me.

"Do you want a baby bird?"

"What?" I said.

"Do you want a baby bird? I found her floating in the water. She's over there. I set her in the sun."

My heart lurched. My God, I thought, it's a nice day, but not warm enough for a drenched bird! I ran over to the little wet spot at the other end of the float. And that's all she was . . . a wet spot. She had no feathers save for several dozen beginnings of quills and a thin coating of yellow baby fluff.

I quickly scooped her up into the warmth of my hands. She hardly seemed to notice. She was cold and stiff, and her tiny body barely filled my palm. Please don't be dead, I thought, please don't be dead! One thin eyelid quivered in response to my silent plea.

It was close to quitting time, so I took an early leave. I called to my dog, Grey, who accompanied me wherever I went, and showed him the tiny creature in my palm. He gave the baby bird a quick lick. I asked Grey to jump in the back of the truck, then I wrapped the bird in an old toque and placed her on the passenger seat. We headed for home.

I phoned the Wildlife Rescue Association. They put me in touch with one of their volunteers, a bird specialist. After I described the creature, she said she was positive it was a pigeon. She told me to boil some chicken eggs, mash the yolks and mix them with enough water to produce a thin, pancake-batter–like consistency. "They come from an egg so it should be okay to feed them egg," she said. "If you can get it into her!"

"What's the problem?" I asked. "Won't she just open her mouth when she's hungry?"

"No, pigeons are different from most other birds. They put their beaks and heads into the parent's mouth, and the parent regurgitates food from its crop directly into the baby bird."

"Hmmm. Thanks for the info." I hung up the phone. How was I going to duplicate that?

The next day, I took the bird to work with me in a small cardboard box lined with rags. The box had a lid that closed out the world and all its dangers and kept in the warmth, a factor important for all babies. Grey Dog kept a close watch on that box.

I left the baby bird in the wheelhouse of the tender boat that served as our coffee shack and lunch room. Every chance I got, I ran over to the tug, opened the box and tried to get that baby bird to eat. She did not respond.

On the second day, I began to feel an anxious knot developing in my insides. This can't go on, I thought. You need food! The boss asked me several times to get my priorities straight and think more about my job. I had only one priority by then: to save the ugly little thing in that box of rags.

For the rest of that day, I practically stood on my head for the bird, but she still wouldn't eat. By the day's end, the anxious knot was in my throat. "You're going to die," I whispered at the helpless little thing. "Damn it!" I pursed my lips and sucked in some air, which squeaked between my teeth. Trying to keep back tears of frustration, I pursed my lips again.

All of a sudden, Birdy stood straight up on her spindly little grey legs and started a shrill squeal. I put my index finger close to her and she began to run her tiny beak across it as if searching. Then I remembered the crop thing. All I could think to do was to put the egg-mix in my hand and, by curling up my fingers, make a container, leaving an opening at the thumb and index finger. With yolk and water running out from between my fingers, I offered the fleshy contraption to the baby bird. She beaked her way to the opening and then jammed her head into my fist. I tipped my hand so that the mixture would run into her, and she guzzled and stuffed herself like the starved creature that she was.

I was elated! She *ate*! She would live! I put the lid back over the rag nest, went out of the wheelhouse and was about to dance a little jig on the float when my boss appeared. "Well?" he said, in a monotone.

"She ate!" I squealed. "She ate! She ate! She ate!"

"Let me see it."

I opened the box to expose the naked, egg-encrusted little beastie inside.

"What is it?" he said.

"It's a pigeon."

"A pigeon!" he exclaimed. "Why couldn't it have been an eagle? A bloody pigeon!" And he walked away.

Birdy became my main focus for the next several weeks. I found a small plastic pill container that would fit in my fist, and that became a makeshift parent's crop. After a week or so, I no longer had to make a fist. Birdy would stick her head directly into the container and I would up-end it, dumping the mixture into her and onto her, filling her ears and eyes as well as her gullet. A warm shower after the evening meal became a daily ritual. When I had her on the job site, we had to make do with a simple sponge bath.

The baby pigeon grew quite rapidly. Eventually, her feathers came in and she looked like a real bird. She began to get steady on her feet, so I occasionally let her follow me around. Grey Dog always kept an eye out for cats, sporting dog that he was, so Birdy was quite safe in that regard. Everyone got used to me driving up with a dog in the back of the truck and a bird in a box on the passenger seat. My two creature friends went everywhere with me.

I remember the first time Birdy flew. I had just climbed up the ladder on the tug that leads to the bridge. Birdy jumped into the air and came along. Then she sat on the upper rail and begged for food, totally unaware of the huge event that had just taken place in her life. I was so proud, you'd have thought I taught her the skill myself!

After a few months, Birdy didn't need her box any more. She had become very independent and adventuresome and flew around a lot. But she always came back to me, and to Grey Dog, who had become her best four-legged friend. I would often see them sleeping in the sun together, Grey Dog stretched out flat on his side, Birdy on top of him. She also ate out of his dish, which he didn't really appreciate, and evening would find her snuggled up to him on his mat under the kitchen table.

When Birdy was old enough, I made her sleep outside at night on a ledge above my bedroom window. At 7:15 every morning she would come in the window — I always left it open a few inches — and sit at the bottom of my bed. Then she would sneak up towards the head of the bed, cooing and chortling her good mornings, finally coming to a resting spot on either my chest or my back. From this position, she would nibble on an ear or nose, or whatever was handy, until I was compelled to wake up and pet her.

One evening, Birdy refused to sleep on her ledge. I had set her out as usual, but less than an hour later she was banging on the window with her wings and beak, obviously in extreme panic. *Let me in! Let me in!* I can only assume that a night predator of some sort had narrowly missed making a meal of her, for she absolutely refused to stay outside again. Instead, she chose the top of the open door between the kitchen and the hallway. The only inconvenience was having to lay newspaper at the base of the door to catch her droppings. Her buddy, Grey Dog, slept in the kitchen at night too. Perhaps the two had cooked up this scheme in order to be together? After Birdy moved in to sleep at night, she would often stay up late. She would jump down from her perch atop the door, walk through the hall to the living room and sit on my lap while I watched TV or read a book, and she'd coo contentedly while I stroked the soft feathers on her back.

Before Birdy came into our lives, Grey Dog's favourite sport had been chasing pigeons along the waterfront. After she came along, it continued to be his favourite sport, only now he had someone to share his game. Whenever he'd spot a flock of pigeons, he would race off in their direction, and Birdy would race off with him, flying right beside him at shoulder height. This pair of waterfront heavies was never satisfied until every last pigeon was on its way. The only thing Birdy didn't do was lift her leg and pee, as was Grey Dog's arrogant custom after a good chase.

We all enjoyed a walk in the country or at the beach. The three of us would often pile in the truck, Grey Dog in the back, Birdy on the passenger headrest and me driving, and we'd head for a place less manicured than the usual city haunts. Grey Dog would hang his head out the canopy window and let the wind whistle through his ears while his pigeon pal clung to her headrest and leaned into all the corners like an experienced motorcyclist. These things did not go unnoticed by other motorists. Birdy often received honks, smiles and waves of recognition. Birdy remained as aloof as the queen, however, never bothering to acknowledge such silly reactions to her presence.

When we finally found a suitable walk site, Birdy always got out of the car and walked beside me. Grey Dog was sent on cat patrol. The words "Get the cat!" sent him on a zigzag pattern of circles around us as Birdy and I strolled along. I would point out different plants to her and she would taste them. I was never sure just what I should be including in Birdy's education.

Birdy even accompanied Grey Dog and me on a cruise from Vancouver to Ocean Falls. She would ride wherever she pleased on the boat, and sometimes she would fly beside it. At night she slept on the wheel, a newspaper placed strategically beneath her.

When we stopped over in Lund for a couple of days, Birdy learned to bug crows. She had never liked crows and would often shudder when she saw one. It is likely that crows were the cause of her being found in Coal Harbour in the first place. So there was no love lost between the two, and she took great delight in harassing them. She would fly high above the Lund Hotel, next to the harbour, and do her best rolls and tumbles, which seemed to incite the crows to riot. Once she had attained the desired level of feathered frenzy, she would race back towards the boat with a dozen angry crows in hot pursuit. At full speed, she would arrive at the galley door and, with the most articulate control, alight on the edge of the door, a feather in a gentle morning breeze. The crows, however, fairly collided with the rigging on the boat. Birdy would take a five-minute breather and then continue the cycle once more.

One day, Birdy decided to nest. She chose my bed in which to lay her eggs. Nesting birds are very hygienic about their nests, so I didn't have to worry about droppings. She also protected the nest quite vigorously from any intruder other than myself or Grey Dog. If company came over and they dared enter my bedroom, they were met with a rage of wing snaps and good sound pecks. I tried, once, to move her nest to a cardboard box in the living room. She would have none of this nonsense, registering her protest by flying straight at the top of the closed bedroom door and beating it with her wings while clawing and kicking her feet.

I began to read up on pigeon behaviour. First and foremost, Birdy was missing a mate. She could lay as many eggs as she wished, but they would never hatch. It was obvious that she considered either me or Grey Dog to be her mate. I knew she would never consider a pigeon. They were things one chased. One did not live with them. But she was getting very crabby waiting for her eggs to hatch.

I phoned my contact at the Wildlife Rescue. It was perfect timing. A proper pigeon couple were being evicted from a balcony in Vancouver, and Birdy could have one of their fertilized eggs.

Birdy accepted the new egg as her own. And after a reasonable duration, the egg hatched. Birdy was ecstatic! She didn't even protest when I attempted to move her to the living room again. There were more important things to worry about, like hiding the eggshells in a faraway place to throw off predators. I took out all the dud eggs. Birdy couldn't have cared less. She was busy caring for her baby, doing all the things the book said she should.

We were a very happy family for three days. On the fourth morning, I got up to find the baby dead. Birdy just sat there, oblivious to this unfortunate fact. Perhaps she was waiting for the little thing to wake up. There was nothing in the book about this. I decided to take the baby bird out of the nest. I showed it to Birdy, trying to make her understand, then I took it outside and buried it in the garden. In retrospect, this was a big mistake. Birdy waited for an hour or so on the nest, and then she started looking. She walked all over the house and called to her baby. It was the strangest sound I ever heard from her, definitely questioning and most certainly nervous. She called and walked and called and walked. She looked under the bed and under the desk. She looked in all the dark corners. She searched and searched for her lost chick. Her calls became wails of desperation. I could not console her or distract her from her purpose. I could only watch with tears in my eyes and agony in my chest. Birdy's heart was breaking.

The next day, Birdy was not our Birdy any more. She was angry and confused. She'd come and sit on my lap and then suddenly lash out at me, pecking and biting and hitting me with her wings. Grey Dog fared no better. Perhaps she finally understood that there was more out there than we, her only family to this point in her life, could give. She had seen what should come from an egg, and it looked nothing like us.

It wasn't long until Birdy left us. I waited for her to come home, but she never did. I left my bedroom window open, just in case.

Snooper
Sharon Arundel

On March 27, 1986, my uncle, who lived on the Sunshine Coast, was in perfect health for a seventy-five-year-old man. That night he phoned his ex-wife long distance in the middle of the night to tell her he was upset and unable to sleep because he'd been wakened three times by a loud breathing sound coming from the corner of his bedroom. My aunt thought awhile. "Where did Snooper used to sleep?" Snooper was my uncle's beloved sheepdog, his companion of seventeen years who had died a few years earlier. My uncle replied, "Well, come to think of it, that was Snooper's special corner."

Feeling somewhat comforted he went back to bed, undisturbed for the rest of the night. Two days later we were shocked to learn my uncle had died suddenly of a heart attack. There is not one member of our family who to this day doesn't believe that somehow, some way, old Snooper had returned from the other side, perhaps to be there to help my uncle across.

Needle in a ...
Judy Hill

Twenty years ago I lived in the upper storey of a creaky old house in which several things happened that were out of the ordinary. Some defied logical explanation altogether, while others prompted the uneasy observance, "My goodness, what a coincidence..."

One November night, as the wind whistled through the spaces under the doors of the frame house, a few of us were sitting in the glow of a small lamp in the high-ceilinged living room. Ivan, who lived downstairs, was at that time very interested in the paranormal. He had recently had us all (sceptics and believers alike) using Ouija boards, and we had spent many evenings in heated discussion of extrasensory possibilities.

That night, however, the topic was a comfortable one — we were telling pet stories. When it was Ivan's turn, he told us of something that had happened to his family cat when he was a boy.

One day, he recounted, he noticed that his cat hadn't been seen for some time, and after a thorough search, he found her huddled under a dresser. As he lay on the floor, trying to coax her from her hiding place, she coughed. Gently pulling her out, he opened her mouth — and wedged in the bony tissue at the roof of her mouth was a threaded needle.

The cat had apparently been intrigued by the thread that hung from the pin-cushioned needle and had, bit by bit, swallowed the thread and the needle that followed. The vet who saved her life said that if the needle hadn't been removed, the cat would have swallowed repeatedly until the needle worked its way down, eventually killing her.

We shivered. None of us had ever heard of such a thing; and at the end of the evening, as my friends went out into the dismal fall night, they all agreed that Ivan's story had been the most bizarre.

The next morning was a typical one. I was running around getting ready for work, feeding and organizing the kids for the day-care centre, doing a last-minute touchup with the iron on a blouse for work, all the usual things. As I finished with my iron in the sewing room, I noticed my delicate black-and-white cat Vicki underneath the dresser where I stored pieces of material. It wasn't one of her normal places, but as any cat owner knows, finding new favourite spots is an ongoing creative process for a feline. I was just about to turn out the light, my mind already on the day ahead, when Ivan's story came back to me.

I bent down and peered at Vicki in her spot under the dresser. She looked back at me, making no sound. Wryly chiding myself for wasting valuable morning time to check out something so silly, I gently pulled her out and opened her mouth. There at the back of her throat was the glint of metal I think I had known would be there.

Later, the vet said she would have died very painfully if I had gone to work that day without looking in her mouth. In the twenty years since, I have never heard of anything like that happening to a cat. In the twenty-four years of my life at that time, I hadn't heard of it either — except for Ivan's story the night before. Not the night after, or five years after — the night before.

My goodness, what a coincidence...

Rabbits May Be Harmful to Your Health

Brian D. Oberquell

Most people, when asked to describe a rabbit, would say something on the order of "a shy, timid forest creature"; however, these people haven't met my pet rabbit, Toby, who sent me to the emergency room of Royal Columbian Hospital in December of 1992.

It was about two weeks before Christmas. I had caught a cold that had developed into bronchitis, and I was sucking on a menthol cough drop as I got down on the floor to play with Toby, forgetting one important fact: RABBITS LOVE MINT AND MENTHOL.

The first (and only) hint of trouble was that Toby's head came up and he seemed more alert than usual. I didn't have time to react when a furry blur hit my face, and then there was a sharp, stinging sensation in my nose. I put my hand up to my face and it came away covered in blood. Toby had bitten me right where you would pierce the nose to put in a ring. After putting a compress on it to stop the bleeding (and having to explain to my wife that she should get off the phone because I was hurt), I looked in the mirror and realized that the wound would probably need stitches.

My wife drove me to Emergency where, as luck would have it:

1. I was the only patient there that evening.
2. The admitting nurses were both Monty Python fans and knew all of the dialogue in *Monty Python and the Holy Grail*, including the scene with the killer rabbit — a fact they demonstrated by reciting the lines with obvious delight.

3. The same nurses wrote on the admitting form that I had been "nipped by pet rabbit," which I felt wasn't very accurate; the triage nurse, however, took one look at the wound and changed "nipped" to "lacerated" (which, for some reason, made me feel better).

4. The doctor who was going to stitch me up called his colleagues over to watch, and asked me if I had any preference as to the colour of the stitches.

5. My wife, trying to be supportive about the stitches, told me that "from a distance they look like nose hair."

I was then faced with the prospect of going to work the next day and having to explain over and over what had happened. A preemptive strike was called for. I sent out a memo over the office E-mail system explaining what had happened so as to head off the queries. But it backfired — nobody had noticed anything until after they had read the memo, at which time they would come over to stare at my nose!

I won't go into what I went through at the company Christmas party a week later. However, I will point out that I still had my cold, and I now know from experience that it is impossible to blow your nose with four stitches in your septum; all you can do is blot with a tissue and pray that you don't sneeze!

As for Toby ... he's healthy and doing fine. Most people don't understand why he's still living (the usual comment is something on the order of "I'd have thrown him in the stew pot"). But I know he wasn't going after me in an aggressive manner (after all, he did let go of my nose when he realized that what he was biting wasn't menthol!), so I don't hold a grudge. I now make sure that, if I'm sucking on a cough drop, I don't get my face near his — and you have to admit, it does make one heck of a story now that I can look back at it and laugh.

On the other hand, I think my wife still holds it against him that he didn't bite all the way through so she could put a ring in...

Zip: A Life
Robert Harlow

He would have lived much differently if he'd lived now. These days, dogs are tied up, fenced in, taken to obedience schools, walked on a leash and neutered. But he lived in a time when freedom wasn't an issue; it was a condition. There was no vet in town. Food didn't come in cans. There was a soup bone — brought home at no extra cost from the butcher store — that simmered in an aluminum pot on the back of our wood-and-coal range, and its marrow, and attached fat and bits of meat, produced a stock that was poured over heels of bread and scraps from the table once a day. He slept at night on gunnysacks in a closed-in space under the steps at the back of our house. He roamed when he wanted to, had friends he hung out with, as well as the self-appointed job of taking John, my youngest brother, to school and back each day in the fall, winter and spring, or to the river to swim in the summer.

Zip was born as part of a litter of four at a way station on the north line of the CNR that runs between Red Pass and Prince Rupert the week the Dionne quintuplets were birthed in 1934. Half springer, half cocker. The bitch's owner had a ten-year-old son — whose character need not be analysed here — who decided he wanted to be the one to crop the pups' tails. He grabbed the smallest, put him on the chopping block and axed off his spaniel tail right at the dog's rump. He whined afterward that he thought it would grow back.

Six weeks later, our father, who worked on the railway, dropped in on his way by. Like many silent New Englanders, he was a sentimentalist. He asked for the pup who had no tail to wag and got him at a reduced price: free. At the time, there was a cute little comic strip running in the *Province* newspaper about a dog named Zipper. Five-year-old John, who normally employed as few words as his father, began to dance up and down, shouting, "Zipper, Zipper."

We had an old dog at the time, Tam O'Shanter, a West Highland white terrier, who came into the house, sniffed Zip, picked him up by the scruff and headed for the door. Tam had been independent to the point where he was almost invisible as a family dog, and when Zip was rescued from him, he growled at us all and left home. The alarm went out, and when an acquaintance brought him back days later, Tam refused to come in or eat. After some anguish, brought on by morally required guilt and a unanimous vote, we took him to live with another old Scot named McIntosh at a lake six miles east of town. Later, my father visited them. Tam sniffed at him as if he were a stranger. Still later, McIntosh bought a Model A Ford pickup and the two of them went on a holiday, drove from their small lake in northern B.C. to the 1939 World's Fair in New York and back. Tam's second life was not so long as his first, but with someone also from the Highlands for a friend, it was happier.

Zip was a relief from Tam's Presbyterian regime. He was a consummate lover, and the world always has too few of those. In lieu of a tail, he wagged his complete back end at everyone, strangers included; but who needed a watch dog in our very small town? (Prince George then had a population of maybe 2,000 if you counted sundry livestock.) When Zip was old enough, he learned to live outside, as we believed then that animals should, and had a life of his own, as well as being a devoted family dog.

Gradually, he became closer to our youngest brother than to anyone else. John was a quiet kid, and often liked to play alone. Zip kept him company, walked him to school, sometimes stayed there, but most often he dozed on the back porch until, at a quarter to three, he'd get up and head down over the hill behind our house, take the path through the woods that bordered the playgrounds and arrive at King George the Fifth Elementary just as the doors opened and the boys ran out of its south end and the girls fled from its north exit.

As Zip's charge got older he began to range farther away from home after school and during the summer holidays. For kids it was in many ways a safer time to grow up — the world was less crowded, expectations were fewer and human horrors not so often perpetrated — and I suspect benign neglect was basic to our upbringing. The river ran at twelve miles an hour, the cut banks above it were steep, but I don't recall anyone drowning. Trees were there to climb. The caves we dug were elaborate, at least by our standards, and their rooms furbished to entice girls to play house were always in danger of collapse. The slough that almost surrounded the town, and was often swum in, was probably polluted about the way the planet is now, but beyond being told often to be careful, there were no restrictions, and pets followed the action wherever it was happening.

Zip became just a dog, flop-eared, black with white patches. His lack of tail stopped being an issue and his personality was no longer remarked on. That's what happens in life: you get taken for granted.

One day, John and a friend decided to explore the abandoned coal elevator, which stood unpainted and weathered on the north side of the rail yards and not far from the roundhouse where the railroad's rolling stock was serviced and repaired. Zip went with them. They walked through the roundhouse and watched mechanics take the drive wheels off a huge steam engine. When the foreman told them to go, they headed on out into the yards and along the last passing track to the old coal elevator.

They went up the stairs and stood on the deck where the coal was once brought for loading onto waiting coal cars. From the edge of the deck they could look fifty feet down the shaft to where the coal used to be stored. Nothing remained at the bottom except a pool of oily water. Not a very interesting place. They went down the stairs and brought up rocks (it was 1940) and dropped them like British bombs into German waters below. They went again and brought more. Bored, they moved on, and somehow, Zip missed them leaving, might have thought they'd gone higher in the elevator or had somehow gone over the edge of the deck and down the shaft. He waited.

Because he wasn't always at young John's heels and had business along the way on every trip they made, he wasn't missed until dinnertime, and not much was thought of it then. But by bedtime, there was concern, and the next morning real worry. The fact was, John didn't remember when he'd last seen Zip. After the elevator they had gone to play on the culverts set out in rows at the cement plant. It wouldn't have been much fun for a dog there.

Two days later, a woman driving by heard a high-pitched noise and stopped her car. It came from the elevator, and she climbed up and found Zip on the darkened deck. She lit a match and saw who it was, talked to him, but he wouldn't budge. When she reached to pick him up, he made very unfriendly noises. She called in to my father's office on the other side of the rail yards and told him where Zip was. Zip cried and growled at him too. It seemed best for Zip if John were taken out of school and driven to the elevator so he could take Zip home. Afterward, young John was very silent for a very long time. Dogs in stories waited — sometimes died waiting — for masters who had disappeared. It was a powerful revelation that it sometimes happened in real life. His own dog would have died. Just for him alone.

Down over the hill behind our place were three houses, two of them hardly more than shacks. Into the one closest to us there moved a family who had been more than normally ill-used by the Great Depression. They were strangers from somewhere away. The two children, girls, were not comely, the mother house-kept as if she were waiting for her own mother to come and do it, and the father was too old to join up and go to war, which might have been a partial solution to their economic problems. And they had a dog, a spaniel, black with white patches, a runt. The family was often not fed, and Lily, the dog, suffered. The father had a temper; he beat his wife and daughters and kicked the dog. Domestic problems were thought then to be nobody's business. Zip didn't know that. He visited, played with Lily and mated with her.

One evening at the end of the summer, Zip came home limping; he shook his head and sneezed a lot. Dirt was up his nose and he had a small cut on his left lower jaw. He wouldn't let anyone touch it, so we knew it was also bruised. What proof was there that the neighbour had done it? We thought of tying Zip up, but that would be as cruel as the beating he'd taken. He lay on his gunnysacks, and our John stayed with him until bedtime.

At breakfast the next morning we saw Zip through the window. He went out of the back gate and down over the hill. It was Sunday. Church was soon. John got up from the table and ran after him. He went to the top of the hill and then we saw him halt. Not unsure; he just stood there waiting. In a while Zip appeared with Lily limping, perhaps staggering, close by his side. Her wretched little body hadn't an ounce of fat on it; her pregnancy was very near to term, and her teats looked as if they were touching the ground. We went outside and watched while Zip took Lily to the entrance of his doghouse under the steps. She went in, and he lay down with his head inside the entrance.

Zip's young master was eleven. He was tall and going to be a big man. Tears weren't any longer on his agenda. The tension needed to be broken. Our father spoke with a fogged voice. "Look at the silly mutt, he's in love."

Perhaps he was. Dog therapists today might have myriad other answers, including the one that says Zip's behaviour was no more than normal among animals. If so, then it was good for some humans to see it. He graduated from dog to mentor, but he didn't become a father. Lily died trying to get her pups born. The man came when our father went to fetch him, and he sobbed when he saw Lily and accused us of killing his dog. We stood and watched. What could we say? He was a man who was terribly hurt, but it was life, not Lily's death, that had done it. Zip went down the hill to sniff and scratch at where the man buried Lily, and he had to run for his life when he was caught doing it. He was never Zip again. Maybe he was terminally hurt too. And angry. He began chasing cars. About a year later, one of his big floppy ears got caught in the wheel of a pickup truck, and it dragged him under and shipped him somehow out the other side. He howled all the way back to the front porch, gave up chasing cars, and the ripped ear healed. He growled at people he decided he didn't like, and once a young girl from grade school accused him of biting her. We found that hard to believe. Owners do. His bird-dog mouth was so soft it hardly appeared possible that he could bite anything but a piece of bread soaked in broth.

John became a teen-ager and began a new kind of life, not of much interest to a seven-year-old dog. Zip became closer to our father, rode with him in his car when he could and sat in the boat at the lake when our father fished. He began to remind us of Tam O'Shanter.

From the beginning, Zip's life had been real. Any sentimentality there'd been in it had all been on the side of his humans. He'd tried his damnedest to be his own kind of dog and had done well. I was overseas, in 1944, when I got a letter from my mother with actual tear stains on it. Our father only an hour before had shot Zip. Cancer of the jaw. It was a decision he'd had to make and a deed he'd had to do by himself, with his own gun. It was what you did then. She said she'd never seen my father cry before, and I don't remember that she ever cried before that either.

Zip passed at ten. Now he might make fifteen comfortably. A dog's life is less free now, but whose isn't? And there's something to be said for vets and canned food and balanced diets.

The Life and Times of Basil and Rosemary, High-Society Finches

Sandra Bette Yates

Rosemary and Basil came home in a cardboard box that sat on the floor of the car, and from the sounds of things, they flew every bit of the way. I released them into the tall, round cage we had bought (not the right shape for society finches at all, but it was on sale) and they began their life with us: my three-year-old daughter, my husband and me.

Their cage was set on a low bookcase near the kitchen table, so we spent a lot of time together. They frittered about the cage, constantly on the alert for food and large predators. I had to admire their "live life in the moment" attitude — every day seemed fresh and new to them, and they never seemed at a loss for something to do. It was truly astonishing, in fact, to realize what a lot of trouble a couple of birds could get into in such a small space, and how much drama they seemed to have in their lives. It helped me to have a finer appreciation for human beings' propensity for entanglements, given that we have a much broader scope of action!

For instance, one day I looked in to see Basil hanging upside-down by one toenail from the side of the nest. He was quite calm, as though trying to give the impression that he was hanging about like that out of his own free will and could right himself whenever he wanted. He bit my finger quite viciously (for a finch) when I freed him. Needless to say, he wasn't any happier about the nail clipping that ensued.

An oversize feeding bin served Basil and Rosemary for a bath, and it was a lot of fun watching them do their daily ablutions. Basil was the more vigorous of the two in his cleaning ritual. He would climb down into the bath until he was submerged up to his neck, and then begin a wild tarantella with his wings, spraying water in all directions. Rosemary soon caught on to this and perched strategically on the edge of the tub, enjoying a dignified and thorough shower for free. When Basil had achieved the degree of sogginess that satisfied him, he would emerge and sit, dripping, on a perch, while he tried to put his feathers back into place. He cut quite a comic figure, as he could simply never do a thing with his hair! The feathers on his head stood straight out at various odd angles until they eventually dried and fell flat again. If Rosemary considered his undignified appearance at such times a matter for ridicule, she never showed it. In fact she seemed to quite dote on the fellow, and they often stood about in an intimate sort of way while they dried off.

We provided them with a nest soon after we got them, because we couldn't stand to see them clinging pitifully to a perch while they slept. We chose an open wicker basket and attached it high up in the cage with twist ties. They loved it. They spent a lot of time there: dozing, preening, pushing one another over just a bit, peering out at the world. This new experience seemed to broaden them, somehow, like travel does with humans. They seemed so cosmopolitan with their cosy little high-rise apartment.

One day, sipping a cup of tea and skimming the newspaper at the kitchen table, I suddenly became aware of an unusual silence and lack of activity from Rosemary and Basil. I could see them in their nest, but somehow they didn't look right. A wave of panic seized me as on closer inspection I realized that they were showing alarming signs of extreme lassitude, their heads lolling drunkenly to one side. To my horror I realized that their water dish and their bath dish were bone dry.

Normally very conscientious about keeping their cage clean and all their supplies topped up, I had been distracted the last couple of days with personal concerns. (You may recall the "broader scope" I mentioned earlier with respect to human entanglements. Sigh. It had been a week like that.) And now, here were my two wonderful friends almost dead from lack of water!

Filling a dish with water, I held it to their beaks. They eagerly began to nibble at the water, weakly at first, and then with more strength of purpose. Within a few minutes Basil was stirring with life and energy. Rosemary was a little slower to come around, but within fifteen minutes both of them were up and about, setting the nest and cage in order, as though looking after the things that they had let slide (tsk, tsk!) during their debilitating illness.

Not long after that, Rosemary began laying eggs. Finch eggs are tiny and perfect, like Scotch mints except indisputably egg-shaped. They inspire awe. When she had a clutch of seven of these marvels, she and Basil settled down to serious domestic duty. She sat on those eggs night and day, Basil spelling her off occasionally while she took in food and drink. Fourteen days later the eggs began to hatch, and out came — five spiders!

Well, technically they were finches, but they looked far more like spiders than birds, all pink with long, scrawny, featherless necks, legs and wings groping about randomly. They made an eerie sound, not very audible at first.

Rosemary tended to the needs of her unlikely looking babies night and day. Their open mouths seemed like strange flowers set atop their spindly necks, and they were open a lot! Tongues wagging, emitting their tiny piercing cries, they pushed and jostled one another for food, food and more food. Rosemary flew back and forth with bits of nestling mush that she thrust into whichever beak beckoned the most insistently. The sounds of her little ones' hunger drove her on and on; the higher the pitch, the faster she flew. Basil made some ineffectual attempts to participate, but he didn't seem to really understand what was required, and he certainly didn't feel any sense of urgency the way Rosemary clearly did. He fussed over them and flew about, touching them gently with his beak as he snuggled next to them, but he didn't participate in feedings as Rosemary did. Perhaps she discouraged him somehow.

When the babies had been satisfied their mouths fell shut and they grew quiet and dozed together, like a heap of wrinkled and deflated old balloons, lovingly clucked over and nuzzled by their parents. Then they would suddenly stir, and in an instant set up their clamorous row all over again. In only three days they began to look as though there was hope after all that they might be finches.

On the afternoon of that third day, as I sat at the kitchen table lingering over a coffee, I heard a terrible thump, the sound of something quite lifeless hitting the floor of the cage. There lay Rosemary, stone cold dead.

I stared at her in disbelief for some time before I reached in and removed her from the cage. I held her, turned her over in my hand and pondered the wonder of how much of a living thing is made up of the force of life, and how little the physical body actually contributes to the equation. Tears flowed as I thought of how she had exhausted herself so completely caring for her babies. We buried her among the flowers in the garden.

Basil was stunned. He sat for hours, as still as could be. He truly appeared to be grieving, as anthropomorphic as that may sound. After some time he began to move about the cage in a distracted and careless manner that was most unlike him, and eventually he made his way up to the nest, where the little ones were clamouring piteously. He watched them for a while, not seeming to know what to do, then he literally dove in amongst them and began shoving them around the nest.

Soon, he tossed one over the side of the basket and it landed in a tangled heap at the bottom of the cage. Horrified, I left the room and tried to think through what I should do next. When I returned, another tiny body lay beside the first. They were definitely dead, but whether he had killed them or they had died for some other reason before he flipped them out, I couldn't say. I scooped the poor little scraps up and took them out into the garden to join their unfortunate mother.

Basil sat amongst his desperately hungry brood and brooded. Then he seemed to take hold of himself. He suddenly flew off, gathered a mouthful of food and flew back to the nest, stuffing the nutritious paste into the nearest available mouth. This act he repeated over and over again until the three hungry babies were replete and fell silent, huddling together and dozing. Basil fed himself, then went up to join his babies, catching a few winks himself before the next feed.

What a bird! What a dad! Rosemary would have been proud of him. We certainly were. We laughed and smiled and praised and cheered some more. Now you really will accuse me of galloping anthropomorphism, but I believe he felt encouraged by us, and that his resolve to help his babies was strengthened by our delight in him.

From that time on, Basil was a devoted father, feeding his babies on demand and never shirking his duty. He brought those babies up all by himself until they were strong and full-feathered and able to fly and feed on their own. When they were fully independent we gave two of them away and saved one as a companion for Basil. We called her Peaches and she was a lovely, sweet-tempered little soul, even though she did hog the bathtub, much to Basil's annoyance.

Although Basil grew irritable in his old age and pecked at poor Peaches for the merest infraction (perhaps the bath issue grew and grew between them, the way different techniques for squeezing the toothpaste can come between human couples), he lived a pretty good life, I think, after all that work of bringing up a family single-handed.

We went away for a week, on vacation, and left Basil and Peaches with another family. Just hours before we returned, Basil died.

Basil joined Rosemary in the garden; we were sad to have lost him, happy to have known him. Good-bye, Basil. (Hello, Rosemary, I can almost hear him say.)

Assistant Mother
Carrie R. Jewell

When I first saw her she was sitting alone on a hill. She seemed to be waiting for us, but how could she have known we were coming? When I stopped the car and got out she climbed in. She went into the back seat, wrapped herself around my three-year-old son and hugged him tightly. I am sure that I couldn't have dragged her out of there. The really funny thing is that, after that day, it took me over six months to get her to enter a car willingly. She was so afraid she would lose her home again.

Lady Lisa was an eleven-month-old Lassie-type collie. She was black with a white ruff, white feet and a white tip on her tail. She had rust-coloured cheeks and eyebrows, and some rust trim on her legs. Lisa had given birth to fourteen puppies when she was eight months old and raised eight of those pups while she herself was still a puppy. At ten months old, after the pups were sold, she was given away. Lisa had lived for only a month at the place where we met her after answering a classified ad. She was being given away again because "Big dogs eat so much." Lisa had very short, dry, brittle hair. She was malnourished and a total emotional wreck.

Being an emotional wreck qualified Lisa perfectly to fit into our small family. We were wrecks too. I was twenty-nine and getting a divorce. We had relocated to a rural community near Salmon Arm, B.C. We did not have much furniture or many toys, but we did have lots of love to give each other, and Lisa too.

Mickie and Lisa were instant pals. She joined in his favourite games, like soccer ball kick and spider catch. In our old log house there were lots of spiders. Mickie liked to drive his big Tonka dump truck around, catch spiders and load them in. One time I counted seventeen of them in the truck. When he had a load he would drive them out the door and dump them in the dirt. Lisa's nose would be inches away as the spiders scattered. It was funny to watch. Another game was doggie-tail crack the whip. Mickie would hold onto Lisa's tail and she would go just fast enough to make him run and be slightly off balance. He laughed and squealed as she ran through the house and around corners. She had the most foolish smile on her face, and her eyes were full of mischief.

When we went outside, Lisa was by Mickie's side constantly. She helped to build snowmen and tried to pull the toboggan when he was sitting on it. Lisa watched over Mickie just like a mother. If he fell down and hurt himself, she was always close by to comfort him. If he fell out of his bed at night, she would come dashing into my room to get me.

We adopted a half-grown orange-and-white kitten and named him Sir Tiggles. Lisa thought he was cute, and he thought she was dreadfully scary. He arched his back, spit and yowled at her. She loved him anyway and ignored his foolishness. Within a week, he was sleeping with her to keep warm. One day we heard a cat yowl from way down in the bush. It was a terrible sound, and we knew that we might not see our kitty again. Lisa took off running down the driveway and into the bush, without making a sound, as fast as she could go. In a minute or two we heard her barking quite savagely. A few minutes later Lisa came walking up out of the trees. As she came closer, we could see that Sir Tiggles was walking with her, winding in and out around her front legs. Lisa's look was full of pride. She was a hero!

Our lives had lots of ups and downs over the following years. I was struggling to be a good parent and to deal with past abuse in my life. It was hard work. It might sound silly, but Lisa helped me more than anyone else. She was never critical, so I could talk to her about everything. She would sit and hold my hand, gazing at me with so much love in her beautiful brown eyes. Somehow she let me know that we could keep on trying. She had faith in me. She loved and respected me. I always felt her strength helping me to learn and make better choices.

My second son, Devin, was born in 1983. It was a problem pregnancy, and my son was born prematurely. He was very ill, and we were in the hospital for over three weeks. When we finally came home I knew that Lisa would be happy to see me but I didn't know for sure how she would feel about the baby. I got out of the car alone to greet her. When Lisa saw that it was me she jumped on me, licking my hands and face, then ran all around the yard yipping and yapping with joy. When she finally stopped to catch her breath I got the baby out of the car to show her. This wonderful look of love came over her face, and as I walked into the house she was right by our side. She sat and watched while I changed Devin and nursed him. He was now her baby too. I knew without a doubt that she would die to keep our boys safe.

As Devin grew and developed, Lisa was there by his side. When he lay on a blanket on the floor she would lie near him. He would pull her whiskers and ears, and she would look up with a silly, lopsided smile of bliss. When Devin was ready to learn to walk Lisa was ready to teach him. She would let him pull himself to his feet with handfuls of her hair and then she would take him walking one step at a time, while he held on to her. Whenever he fell they would start over again. She was so patient. It was nice to have Lisa there to share my boys with.

One day Lisa disappeared. She was gone all day. We hunted for her but we didn't find her. When she came home that night she brought a man with her. She had spent the whole day in the hay field with him and then he drove her home in his truck. Bill was a neighbour and we had met once or twice before, but over the next two years our friendship grew. Bill used to plow our driveway, and when he came into the yard with his tractor both Mickie and Lisa made sure they invited him in for tea. Bill and I were married in 1985 and will be celebrating our tenth anniversary this year. We have a happy, loving relationship based on a true friendship. I believe that somehow Lisa knew he was the right man for us.

After Bill and I were married and we settled into our new home, Lisa's job was easier. She still took care of the boys, but she didn't have to take care of me so much. She loved Bill and trusted him. It was comical to watch her when Bill played rough and tumble games with the boys. Lisa would get in between them and Bill, whining and begging him not to hurt her boys. That would usually finish the game because we would all be laughing so hard. But if the boys were actually naughty she would tell on them and then turn her back so she wouldn't have to watch them be punished.

Lisa became very ill in May of 1991. She had a severe infection somewhere in her body. We babied her, gave her medication and prayed for her to get well, and one day she seemed to. She jumped up and insisted on going to get the boys from school. She was so weak I had to help her into the truck. I thought for a little while that she might be getting better, but the next day she was worse. Lisa and I went out for a little walk and she told me with her actions that she wanted to go away and die. I knew then that we had to make a family decision to end her pain and her life.

Mickie and Devin helped to make the decision and were very strong about it. I sat beside Lisa and held her paw while she died. I told her how much we loved her. I remembered all the times she had comforted me in the same way. I felt happy that I was not letting her down when she needed me, but I knew how sad and lonely it was going to be without her. She licked my hand to say good-bye.

I'll never forget Lisa. Because of her I am a person who is strong and confident, more able to make good decisions, more determined to follow my heart and do what is right for me and my family. Every year on Mother's Day one of us puts a bouquet of flowers on Lisa's grave. We remember her with love and laughter. There is a special spot in our hearts that belongs only to Lisa.

Last Tour of Duty
Carol S. Bosier

Duke, the aging miniature schnauzer, had come to take a break with a dying friend at the hospital's extended care unit.

Duke had been on similar missionary missions over the past thirteen years. Duke and I served on pet therapy patrol in hospitals, and in community health, home-care and volunteer work. He had the tenacity, energy, strength and intelligence of his breed, and he spent many hours working and travelling with me in both the U.S.A. and Canada. Our credo was "Compassion, duty and service." Whether you were human or animal made no difference to Duke. We felt more joy than sadness, as our presence gave healing and comfort to others.

Duke had a lot of my personality. And he had an American Kennel Certificate of Pedigree, with a registered name, Duke of Heidelberg. Me, well, I was a registered professional nurse with a degree in my field.

Duke was born November 30, 1976, in Olathe, Kansas. He grew from the "runt of the litter" to a handsome, stocky, salt-and-pepper gent with black eyes that could rivet one's soul and heart. His nickname, "Silver Bullet," fit his colour, spontaneity and speed.

Duke especially loved children, horses, dogs, cats, the elderly and me. He even enjoyed smelling flowers, although probably for their unseen inhabitants and not for their perfume. Whether Duke was racing with horses or with my friend's whippet, or cuddling with a cat, he enjoyed life to the fullest. A mellow fellow! He was a real lap dog and enjoyed cuddling anyone who offered.

On this breezy July day, we were driving to the hospital for our evening shift on pet patrol. Duke rode in his usual shotgun position: two front paws firmly planted on the arm rest of the passenger door, his eyes scanning the neighborhood and his ears and tail pointed straight up like radar.

It was the last visit for Duke at the hospital in Vancouver, where an extended care unit was using pet therapy as part of auxiliary services. He had been a member of the new patrol for almost six months. But Duke was getting fragile, and I knew his aging body soon would force him to retire. He suffered from complications due to heart failure, arthritis, poor eyesight and diminished hearing.

When we arrived, Duke hurriedly acknowledged his comrades in the unit's dining area. Then he split for his friend's room. As I entered the room of the elderly man named Lim, I found Duke with his paws up on the bed railing. He was wagging his stub tail and whining. The bed was elevated up to my waist, and Duke could not see Lim, who was lying semi-comatose.

They had developed a camaraderie over the preceding months. Lim had used a wheelchair due to his stroke residual, but he always had a big smile on his face when Duke came to the unit, and Duke was always welcomed on the old man's lap. They glowed with mutual affection as Lim stroked Duke rhythmically and Duke wagged his tail.

As I watched that wagging tail now, it was plain Duke wanted to see Lim. I hesitated, considering hospital rules and regulations, but since I was the R.N. in charge, I lifted Duke onto the bed. There was an order for a "no code" (meaning no extraordinary measures for prolonging life), and they didn't expect Lim to survive the night. Since he had no family in Canada, it was fitting that his only friend lie down beside him. Duke gently manoeuvred his body close to Lim's and licked the limp, fevered hand of his friend.

No response.

Duke sniffed his friend's white hair and nuzzled Lim's neck with his wet, black button nose. Finally he whimpered in Lim's ear. Lim slowly opened one mucus-matted eye and smiled a faint, one-sided grin. Duke's stubby tail wiggled in recognition of a familiar phantom language. He received a gentle pat on his head from one ghostly hand, and he stretched out his paws to further arouse his friend to play.

Lim's eyes closed, the smile remaining on his face. He took his last laboured breath. Duke, his ears down, stretched his paws out tight against Lim's body. He crawled closer and seemed to bathe in his friend's last energy flow. Like a sentry in the night, he sensed his friend had pulled rank on him this time.

Four months after that last tour of duty, Duke died in my arms. I shall always remember our friendship and the gifts he gave others. Whether standing guard by my bed at night or rising to visit a sick patient or disturbed friend, he never hesitated.

May this brief encounter with Duke be his gift to you.

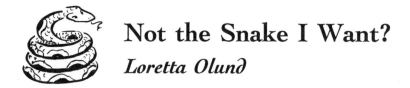

Not the Snake I Want?
Loretta Olund

The animals that I would never buy for myself have, by some quirk, usually become the most interesting of my pets. So it was with Kaa, my baby boa. I am fond of boas. Most are good-tempered, and a full-grown person can manage a full-grown snake on their own. But one thing turned me off these snakes — they ate rabbits. I had had pet rabbits for years and could not bear the thought of feeding one to my snake.

One day while I was working at the pet store someone phoned to tell us that they had found a "python" slithering down the hall of their apartment building. They wanted it out immediately. I told them to bring it to the store.

The husband brought it down in an ice-cream pail, and when I lifted the lid I saw a young boa constrictor. The boa's spine was sticking out, furrows ran the length of her almost two-foot-long body and her skin hung loosely. The poor snake was starving.

I decided to take her to my vet. I could feed her, but if something else was draining her resources she might die. Dr. Prus agreed the snake was emaciated but said the boa showed no other signs of illness. I decided to buy the snake for $50 and give her a second chance. Once she was healthy, I could sell her. At my nephew's suggestion, I named her Kaa, after the python in *The Jungle Book*.

At first I offered Kaa small mice. She took quite quickly to the pre-killed morsels. I kept her warm and gave her lots of fresh water. I began to feed her larger foods, including baby chicks a day or two old. Luckily Kaa needed fat and muscle, and unlike a lot of snakes she accepted the new food without a problem. As Kaa gained weight, I realized that it wouldn't be long before she outgrew the ten-gallon fish tank she was in.

With my mother's help, I converted a secondhand coffee table into the cage that would last Kaa a good part of her life.

Snakes are the Houdinis of the reptile world, and Kaa soon began to show me how escape-proof her cage wasn't. I'd patch up the holes and try again. Kaa never left the bedroom when she escaped. Most times she could be found curled up by the bed, but once I found her in a hat inside my dresser.

I soon learned Kaa liked to be handled. As soon as I put her into her cage she would turn around and climb back onto me or just refuse to let go. She even allowed her head to be stroked and her lower jaw to be pulled down to show people her teeth and mouth. Snakes usually don't care for these things.

Once Kaa was healthy enough, I started to bring her to Association of Reptile Keepers of British Columbia (ARK) shows. Her good-natured quietness and the way she moves so slowly won over many people. They would touch her tail to find out she wasn't slimy after all and would soon hold or pet her. Kaa loved the attention.

Kaa has been with me just over a year. She's muscled up, her skin fits nicely and her bones no longer show. That starving snake changed my life, and I'm glad I've changed hers.

Kaa is never going to eat rabbit, though. Other than that she'll want for nothing. She has taken a liking to slithering around my little house plants, so I've decided that when I get my next pay cheque, I'll buy Kaa an indoor tree.

Luke
LolaDawn Frias

His eyes were very, very sad. Overflowing with immeasurable sorrows. He would not look directly at me, and I understood. At that time, I was also new in this prison. Not sure enough or brave enough to let a stranger see my naked fears.

Luke had been running loose and wild in a park for a year or more. He was used to open spaces. I came from a farm near a small town, and was never in any kind of trouble before. Never caged. All the locked doors weighed heavy on my soul. Heavy on Luke's, too. I could tell from that glimpse of his brown eyes.

I missed my own dog desperately. My dust-mop Shih Tzu had been my constant companion for seven years. He slept on my bed, warm against my legs. Sat by my side through every daily high and low. Listened attentively to all my thoughts. I longed for his presence during the empty nights in my cell.

Dog trainer Kathy Gibson operates a canine program at Burnaby Correctional Centre for Women. I had asked to join her work program, reaching for the open spaces I had been taken away from. Searching for the reassuring sound of wind in the trees instead of banging doors. Alone among strangers, I grasped for any lifeline.

I saw Luke when I toured the indoor kennels. A ragged shepherd-something cross. Patchy fur. Leery ears. Sitting stiffly in the farthest corner of his kennel, willing his bony shoulders to fit tight against the concrete block walls. Too rigid to breathe while I looked through the glass in the locked door. Knowing how he felt, I wanted to cry. I, too, knew that terror!

When I finally met him, I wanted to apologize for breaching his privacy. I wanted to wrap my arms around him, bury my face and wail our shared frustrations. I wanted to say so much to this fellow starving, hurting soul. Instead, I cautiously extended my hand, palm down. Luke shrank inward, the gesture of tense retreat barely perceptible. He stared at the blank wall.

The hope was to rehabilitate Luke and prepare him for an adoptive family in the outside world. But he was frightened into paralysis by a mere leather leash, and I wondered if that dream could ever become reality for him. I wondered, too, if I would ever see my farm and my own little Shih Tzu again.

So I joined the canine workforce, and the daily struggle to drag Luke outside on unwilling feet, tail tucked so tightly between his legs it hugged his belly. He was too worried to drop his guard and lift his leg with a stranger at the other end of the leash he tried to gnaw away. So we allowed him privacy to take care of necessities, putting him on a long line and standing with backs turned, line slack, until he finished. Then we tried to stroll back across the field without sending him into hysterical flight against the high, heavy chain-link fence. Eventually we could trick him back into the classroom by leaving the door open, holding our breath and not moving until he was actually inside and on his blanket. Any unexpected stir and he fled across the yard, trembling in terror, and we had to start all over again.

It was so exhilarating when Luke finally allowed one of us to sit on the edge of his blanket. He stayed, unleashed, eyes rolling, limbs locked, saliva dripping from clenched teeth. Puddled in his own panicked urine. His fear smelled like acidic, decaying fruit in the still classroom. But it was one minuscule step towards better.

He was encouraged to sit on his blanket and experience the classroom, to hear our voices near him and to get to know the terrifying world of gurgling coffee-makers, clattering brooms, swishing washing machines and squawking radios. He shivered and shook, and great handfuls of scruffy hair fell to the floor. We spoke with measured, cheerful voices. Repeated his name again and again. Included him in our conversations. We called and cajoled and teased with light-hearted tenderness. We coaxed and flattered and complimented him.

We tried to tempt him with biscuits by sitting quietly on the edge of his blanket and offering crumbs again and again. We inched bits across the floor with gentle fingers while he remained rigid, staring anywhere except at one of us, the whites of his distressed eyes glaring. The biscuits were lapped up later by other happy dogs. Never by Luke.

Another canine worker finally won the biscuit battle. She persisted patiently until Luke picked up a bite, allowing his lips to come within inches of her hand. He did not eat that piece. He dropped it in his hurry to regain his composure. But she kept offering tidbits of love, and eventually Luke accepted a piece from her open hand.

What a victory! We celebrated with gratified grins. The occasion called for leaping and dancing and shouting triumph to the rafters, but that would have undone Luke's accomplishment, probably set him back beyond redemption. Slowly, very slowly, he let us into his world, allowing us to feed him the biscuits, then to touch him and eventually to brush away the dry, unhealthy hair.

Personally, I cherish the moment Luke met my eyes for the first time. Perhaps it was the song I hummed while I mopped the floor that caught his attention. Maybe he was curious, or finally secure enough to explore his surroundings. He did not like to go near his kennel door of his own accord, so when paws and head appeared I nearly dropped my mop! He looked right at me for one fluttering heartbeat, then cringed back into his usual corner.

There was wisdom in his brown eyes. There was knowledge and experience and goodness. His eyes spoke of his strong desire to be well and to belong. To be wanted. Loved. All the things I needed myself. I had heard the saying "In giving, you receive," and that fleeting glimpse told how much I could receive from Luke. However, to enjoy his gift of friendship, I had to let go of my own barriers.

I wish I could say that happened right away. Unfortunately, we both carried too many bad memories. Ugly internal scars. We both had to learn to trust, to let others in. We tiptoed around each other in cautious circles, giving a little, but never all. Accepting a bit, but never everything.

Our relationship changed on a February evening when neither of us expected it. We were both caught up in a frolicking game of fetch-the-tennis-ball with a lively little beagle cross. I politely offered the ball to Luke, who politely refused it, then threw it for the beagle. Luke ran the other way while she brought it back for another round. The air was crisp, and snowflakes fell like floating feathers in the brightly lit prison yard. The ball soared again and again. I forgot my worries while Luke forgot his concerns.

"BOOF!" I nearly dropped the ball. "BOOF!" from behind me again.

I thought another worker had accidentally let a third dog outside. But it was Luke. Front paws splayed, head down, ears up, tail in the air. Luke had a tail! A beautiful wagging plume! And a voice, never heard before. A deep, handsome voice!

"BOOF!" Again. "BOOF! I want to play, too!" So we played.

Luke left the Correctional Centre in June. His release papers came before mine. He left cheerfully, proud head held high, attentive ears forward. Curious about his new family and looking forward to his future. The lean days in the park and the apprehension over making new friends was finally gone. Luke is living with a good family, and I am pleased to hear he is adapting happily. It was very difficult to say good-bye.

When I am released from this institution, I may choose to keep silent about "being in jail." It has been hard to accept the terms of my incarceration, and it will probably be difficult for the public to accept this fact as well. However, I consider myself extremely privileged to have shared a small space in the excellent canine program. Inmates have the opportunity here to learn basic animal care, obedience training and grooming skills. Even tracking! By handling the dogs, prisoners can learn valuable and essential life skills, such as making good decisions, handling changes and dealing with turbulent emotions. When I am "out," I will be better equipped to accept whatever life has in store.

I cannot wait to hug my own little dog when I get back to the farm. But there is something else I want to do too, something I want to keep from this experience. I am going to hang a photograph above the mantel, a picture of a stray shepherd cross with sad brown eyes.

How I Learned to Speak Dog
George N. Murray

I have never, in my adult life, owned a dog. This is the story of a dog I was privileged to care for, and learn from, many years ago when I lived on the river. I was building my sailboat in a live-aboard community nicknamed Dogpatch on the Fraser River in the late seventies. Sponge (so named because she could soak up any amount of food or affection) was a one-year-old Doberman. When her owner went to South America for five months, I looked after Sponge. It was during this time that I learned to speak dog.

Dogs have a nonverbal method of communication with one another and with any human bright enough to catch on. My communication with Sponge just sort of happened. It began when I noticed that she looked to me for signals on how to cope with anything out of the ordinary. She was treating me as a combination parent/pack leader. The first instance of this occurred when the Franklin stove spat sparks onto the hearth. I stamped them out as a fire precaution. I noticed that Sponge watched my actions carefully. Then she began to stamp the sparks out with her forepaws.

When Sponge's enormous bag of dry dog food ran out, I tipped it so that she could see it was empty. She stuck her head in and emerged with a tragic look. We then walked to the store. As she looked through the window and saw me going through the checkout with a fresh bag of food for her, she sat up and eagerly licked her chops.

I began to understand that Sponge's exaggerated listening gesture, head cocked to one side and then the other, meant, "I don't understand. What do I do now?" This was confirmed one day when I used the gesture to ask *her* a question when she acted fussy and agitated. She ran to the kitchen and dragged out her dish, then sat behind it and looked at me expectantly.

Like a curious child, Sponge always watched whatever I did, seeming to want to learn from me. One day I took my bicycle apart to regrease the crank bearings. Sponge observed as usual. When I began reassembly she looked worried and dejected. Did she fear that she'd never be able to put a bike together herself?

When her owner returned, my unique relationship with Sponge ended. I finished my boat and moved on. Years have gone by since then, and I am sure that my canine friend passed away long ago.

Most Dobermans I've met have been gentle, intelligent creatures like Sponge. I believe that this is their true nature, if they are not trained to be guard dogs. They owe their reputation for viciousness to mistaken folklore.

Bruce
D. C. Kilpatrick

Bruce was our spitz, a dog-about-town, when my family lived in Nanaimo in the early 1920s. A free spirit, he roamed far and wide. He had a strong feeling for his family's welfare and seemed to feel that he had to help to provide food. This caused my parents a good deal of concern when Bruce would bring home chicken eggs and leave them, unbroken, on the back porch. My mother feared that someday he would become the target of an angry chicken farmer with a shotgun.

In the summer of 1926 my family moved to Vancouver. One hot afternoon in mid-July, Mrs. Lyon, our next-door neighbour, was over visiting, sitting on the top step at the front of our house with me, a six-month-old baby, on her lap. About a hundred yards away along our street men were clearing land for the construction of some retail stores. There were some very large stumps in the property since it had been logged not too many years before. The common practice at the time was to blast the stumps out and then burn them.

Suddenly Bruce appeared, running at top speed, coming from the direction of the land clearing. Up the front steps he raced and with hardly a pause grabbed me by my diapers and dragged me through the open front door, down the hall, into the kitchen and under a day-bed in the corner.

Mrs. Lyon screamed to my mother that the dog had gone mad and attacked the baby. In the midst of all this yelling and confusion there was the sharp crack of an explosion, followed moments later by the crash of something striking the roof. It shook the house to the foundations. A large piece of tree stump was embedded in the shingles.

Recalling the incident later, my parents wondered how Bruce knew that this particular charge was dangerous. Blasting was a common occurrence in Nanaimo. The crew had blasted stumps on previous days, and Bruce was in the vicinity. Why did this one alarm him?

Three weeks later, shortly after our roof had been repaired, the same crew were burning the stumps in a strong wind. The flying sparks set our roof on fire — but that is another story.

Peter
Hazel I. Miller

My dad, a pioneer of Nelson, B.C., named Harry Hulls, had as across-the-street neighbours a family whose members loved cats. Amongst their feline coterie was a huge venerable patriarch named Peter. He must have sensed that Dad was an animal aficionado for, every morning without fail, weather notwithstanding, Peter made his way across the street to enjoy the ministrations of Dad's affection for him: some gentle stroking and a round of very satisfying ear scratches.

Since this benefactor's deteriorating eyesight had required that he give up driving, he had become a patron of the city bus service. The neighbourhood bus stop was directly in front of Peter's abode and, no matter what day — or at what hour of the day — my dad went across to catch a bus, Peter was there to see him off. And just as inevitably, no matter what time he came home, Peter was there to oversee his safe progress back across the street.

During several years of this routine, Dad developed what became terminal cancer. He was sent to Vancouver for surgery and died there. From the day that he left Nelson, Peter never again went to Dad's house and he did not ever oversee the departure or arrival back of any city bus.

The funeral was held at the United Church two blocks from Dad's home. Just before the service was to begin, we were startled by the doleful sound, from the back of the congregation, of a series of three or four of the most mournful meows ever heard — and then total silence.

Peter had not come with anyone. But he was there, as always, to see his dear old friend off on his journey.

A Deerhound to Remember
Al Longair

Rob Roy McGregor was the noble companion that I was fortunate to share a few years with before his untimely ending. He came to us as a scrawny twelve-week-old puppy that was anything but cute. Most people likened him to a rat from the *Muppet Show*. He was all legs that went every which way; he was covered with grey, wiry long hair and was almost unnoticeable if you looked at him straight on. A scarecrow looks more fleshed out than a Scottish deerhound puppy! What enamoured him to me was his scruffy coat and his total lack of cuteness. His long legs may also have had some bearing on the decision, as I am personally quite familiar with this situation. All in all, how could anyone not like such a pitiful-looking beast?

We were lucky to have Robbie grow up with us on a small acreage where he was taught by another old faithful canine, Salem, our Afghan/Irish setter cross. These two would run together through the underbrush, coming back with various bits of flora attached to their plumage. Salem was a tolerant tutor even though Robbie grew past him by his seven-month birthday. The two dogs were not inseparable pals, but they shared an existence of mutual respect. Robbie would rather play flat out for twenty minutes a day, then retire to his mattress under the stairs to rest before dinner. He never quite caught on to Salem's love of sitting under a tree silently gazing up into the heights in a most champion-like pose for hours on end trying to will the squirrel down to the ground. (We never knew what Salem would do if he ever really came within ten feet of a squirrel, but he certainly appeared to have plans for something exciting.) Robbie, on the other paw, seemed determined to live a more refined life.

Despite not being cute, you could not call Robbie uncuddly. He loved to be held and sit on your lap. Unfortunately for Robbie, he quickly grew out of being a lap dog, but he devised a simple way to accommodate his inner desire. When Robbie was full grown, he developed the habit of walking up to the side of the chair, then climbing up and over top of the person sitting there to rest his chest on their lap. All four of his feet lightly touched the floor, front paws on one side and hind paws on the other. Most people found this comical to watch, but it could be unsettling for a guest who had decided to sit in Robbie's favourite lap chair!

Deerhounds can grow to almost the stature of their cousins, Irish wolfhounds. His height would get poor Robbie into trouble at times. Food had to be carefully put away; left on counters or stove tops, it would mysteriously disappear without a trace. On one important occasion, a birthday cake was left on top of the freezer in the utility room after many hours of painstaking preparation. Unfortunately, Robbie did not remind us that he was lying in the room to dry off before being allowed into the house proper. By the time the guests started to arrive for the party, the cake was more than three-quarters devoured. This time, however, the evidence of how it met its demise was readily at hand. It was not an easy task to find a replacement birthday cake in a small town on a Sunday afternoon before the liberalization of shopping hours!

By eight months of age, Robbie had become a fixture in our life. He would often not move from his resting place to perform the canine duty of inspecting all and sundry that crossed the threshold, so visitors would be surprised by Robbie groaning from his private space below the stairs or ever so quietly lifting his head to see what would dare consider interrupting his eighteenth nap of the day. He was also a most patient chap; he would put up with our toddler placing inquisitive fingers up his nose or lifting his lip to count his teeth. Because of this trait, he was a natural to succeed Salem and accompany me on my school visits to talk to young children.

Classes from kindergarten to grade six all responded in the same way the first time they met Robbie. He would walk in on the leash to a rumble of oohs and aahs. Some youngsters would back away in fear, but they soon warmed to him even though he towered over most of them. The students liked to see how far up their bodies Robbie's back would reach. After they overcame this initial astonishment, Robbie would walk patiently around the circle of students to introduce himself and allow each child to have a quick pet. He would occasionally grace a child with an endearing quick lick on the nose for good measure, possibly cleaning up remnants of a breakfast or snack. Having done his job, Robbie would plop down in the middle of the circle, preferably on a carpeted floor, and proceed to feign sleep.

I would talk about pet care and responsible animal ownership. If the talk was getting dull, Robbie would try to lie on his back. This was always met with squeals of delight, as his legs would flail in the air and his head was never quite sure which way it should flop. He would squirm around for a bit, then find another pose to strike for the remainder of the visit. During this second half, he would usually have little humans crawling over him, tickling his toes, examining his nostrils and teeth, and looking at his unmentionables, much to the delight of his audience. When it was time to go, he always made a show of how difficult and inconvenient it was to have to get all the way up onto those long legs of his. He would stand for the final hugs and cuddles, and then we would be on our way to the next class to repeat the episode, with minor variations in performance.

Because of Robbie's public profile, he could not be taken to a park or baseball field without some child running over to greet him. They couldn't remember who the heck his human companion was, but they sure knew Robbie! He could be mobbed by little ones and stand there patiently, not basking in the glory but simply standing as if resolved that it was his duty to allow the kids to love him. He was truly a remarkable dog.

In the off-season, Robbie was allowed some holiday time away from his adoring public. It was during one of these times that his first and only swimming lesson took place. The location was the sandstone beach area around Taylor Bay on Gabriola Island. Salem was having a great time chasing after the sea gulls, and Robbie quickly caught on to the fun this could be. When the fateful moment occurred, I had just happened to glance up from the book I was reading.

Chasing sea gulls involved running along the rocks and in the shallow water parallel to the shoreline, then turning and running after the birds again as they rose up and flew back down the beach. The gulls were quite professional in their disdain for canids and played out the game to the fullest. On one of their passes overhead, Robbie turned and ran back along the beach at full speed, then simply plummeted out of sight under the water. The gulls had led him to the edge of an underwater precipice.

Whether this move was premeditated or not is a matter of great conjecture, but it was certainly effective. After what seemed like an eternity, the startled hound lifted himself clumsily out of the water and stood on dry land with a most bedraggled look of bewilderment. Seeing a deerhound in the flesh often raises concern about the owner's ability to provide enough calories for his charge, but seeing one wet is so pitiful it becomes hilarious! The look on his face as he surfaced from the brine is one that I will always cherish. Poor Robbie carefully and gingerly skulked back up the beach to the cabin, plunked himself down and could not be coaxed back to the beach for the rest of the day. In fact, Robbie was so dejected that he never returned to the delights of running along a beach. Those gulls must have had quite a chortle about their successful trick at their gathering that night.

I shall never forget my quiet and loyal companion. His joy and grace while running through a field was a sight of immeasurable beauty. His kindness and gentle way with all manner of folk made him a truly dignified being. In Robbie, his breed's rich and noble Scottish heritage could not be missed. It was quite an honour to have been able to share his life.

I'd Give Them Only Six Months to Live

Hermina A. van Gaalen

The first time I saw Honey and Sparky, two American crested guinea pigs, was in an elementary school classroom almost six years ago. Honey had given birth to three cute little babies that morning; my father, who worked at the school, called home to tell us the news. Three hours later, I was handling the babies and their parents. Honey was petrified due to fear of people and natural maternal instinct. Sparky was indifferent, resigned to fate.

Before my arrival that morning, my father had cleaned the cage, which had not been prepared in any way for the expected event. Mother and babies were now dry, comfortable and hiding away in a box in the cage. When the animals' owner arrived for her class, she showed very little concern about what Honey and her babies had experienced in the wee hours of the morning. The owner of these guinea pigs considered them "just rodents": pieces of "living furniture" that one would occasionally look at, feed when remembered, and ignore most of the time. Many times, especially after a weekend, my father would find Honey and Sparky without food or water, so he would bring vegetables, fill water bottles and talk to them.

My first inclination was to take the whole bunch with me, but this wasn't to be. After they were weaned, the three babies were sold off, and Honey and Sparky were to have two more litters in the following months. The stress of not receiving adequate food between pregnancies showed in Honey's collapsing frame and patchy fur, and in the dramatically smaller babies in the subsequent litters. Since Sparky had an outgoing personality, he received more than his share of being mishandled by some children and adults.

Eleven months after our first encounter, Honey and Sparky, no longer welcome at the school, were to be given to a pet shop. Who would buy these half-starved little blond things? They would probably end up as snake food! That thought alone was enough to make me rescue them. Driving away from the school with Honey and Sparky safely in a carrier box gave our family tremendous relief. Once at home, introductions began. Honey and Sparky already knew and completely trusted my father, for his ever-present help, and he now became their regular baby-sitter. My mother became the one to beg from for a little more bread at breakfast and daily fresh fruit and vegetables. My sister became their nurse and chief manicurist. I became their total caretaker, and they became my babies.

Honey and Sparky were in such poor physical and mental condition that I estimated they would be lucky to live for six months. Sparky responded to the move as would any animal who had experienced only insecurity by constantly changing hands; the previous owner had frequently let schoolchildren take these animals home. Honey was so terrified that, whenever she was held, she lost control of her bowels. It broke our hearts.

Our first few months together were spent trying to reassure Honey and Sparky that they were safe and would receive enough food, have clean cages and, most importantly, be loved and appreciated. The idea that their cages would be cleaned regularly was a new concept for them. For a while, after being returned to his clean cage, a surprised Sparky would check his whole cage, skipping about with delight. Bedding of straw or hay became new sources of entertainment for them. This clean-cage idea restored their natural desire to perform their own personal grooming and be intolerant of soiled living conditions.

From the safety of their cages in the kitchen, Honey and Sparky could oversee the family's goings on. Although they were initially fearful of many typical household noises, the familiar sound of plastic wrapping brought joyful squeaks and cage rattles. They associated that sound with the vegetables my father had brought to them in the school. As time progressed, their opinion of some scary sounds changed: the once-frightening sound of the back door, now welcome, announced the arrival of their favorite garden goodies. However, Honey and Sparky never accepted some sounds, like firecrackers, songs with bells in them and the noises of children.

After living with us for about four weeks, Honey and Sparky took turns exercising outside of their cages. Sparky, frightened of the sudden open area in the living room, was motionless. Within fifteen minutes, though, his curiosity got the better of him, and he started to explore. Upon realizing he was really free, he went absolutely crazy, zipping in circles around the Christmas tree and furniture. When it was Honey's turn, she, predictably, sat paralyzed with fear. Only when she was covered with a familiar box did the freedom bug finally bite her. Then Honey too ran to her heart's content! This playtime brought out their individual personalities: Honey took great pleasure in shoving boxes and cans around or pretending to bite furniture to get attention; then she would mischievously skip away. Sparky loved to explore unknown territory, poke his nose into forbidden places and follow his people like a puppy.

Since Honey and Sparky had lacked the proper nutrition, their appetites initially couldn't be satisfied. They would eat just about any-thing to the point of bursting. On a visit to the garden, Honey spied the onion patch. With eager eyes, she quickly leaped into the patch, then attacked and savagely devoured a large onion stalk. As the "bottomless pits" were slowly filled, the eating of unusual foods stopped. However, Honey never completely lost the survival instinct to quickly munch up her favourite foods.

Daily handling helped break down much of Honey and Sparky's fearfulness and mistrust. My father often had the contented guinea pigs cosily snoozing in an old sweater. Once, while sitting on his shoulder, Honey noticed my father eating a cookie. Before my father could get another nibble, Honey stole a big bite. Honey, by this point, was totally different from the timid creature that had first arrived. Now she was a bold, bright-eyed cutie who would occasionally give me socks in the jaw, her versions of the kisses I had given her. Sparky, knowing he was home at last, now showed his appreciation through his happy skips, beautiful whistles and tiny guinea pig kisses.

The abuse Honey and Sparky had suffered temporarily robbed them of their capabilities and also permanently haunted them. Early one morning Honey heard the familiar sound of my father's keys, which had meant food, water, someone who cared in her early school days. She let out a loud piercing cry. Realizing she was no longer in that dreaded environment, Honey never made that mistake again. Honey and Sparky's bodies never fully recovered. Honey's "saddle" back still showed the tremendous strains of three closely spaced pregnancies. Sparky continued to experience pain by his left hip, which had been damaged when he was dropped from waist height.

Honey and Sparky knew they were very much part of our family. Both had wonderful sweet characters that, although very different, displayed incredible intelligence and love. The complex personality of the guinea pig is underestimated by many an ignorant individual. The previous owner never knew what deep contentment she could have received from these two small, thankful, comical munchkins. That was her terrible loss.

Sadly for us, first Sparky, and then six weeks later Honey, died of old age last fall. My initial estimate of them living for six months had turned into almost four extremely happy years. Rarely a day goes by that I don't wish they were still around to continue to live "only six more months."

A Small Death

Jancis M. Andrews

One day, my daughter came to me with an urgent request. The parents of her boyfriend owned a cottage in Washington State and were upset about a man living nearby, who was continually abusing his dog. Complaints to local authorities had changed nothing. If she and Graham stole the dog, Elaine asked, would I take it in?

My husband, Ian, travelled widely as a sales manager while I stayed home in West Vancouver, juggling the needs of a teen-aged son and daughter, volunteering in the community and attempting to complete my university studies. I knew it would fall to me to exercise and feed the dog and I did not want the extra burden. But all my objections could not erase the image of a battered animal. Reluctantly, I agreed, adding that I would take the dog to our local S.P.C.A.

My grumbling was silenced the minute Elaine and Graham returned. Limping up the driveway was a young, emaciated, part Saint Bernard bitch. Her tail hung between her legs, and her ribs protruded from a filthy, matted, reddish-coloured coat. Huge patches of hair were missing from her back and the raw skin was crisscrossed with crimson weals. Because of the man's repeatedly kicking her, she was deaf in one ear, and one hip was out of joint.

But besides these horrors, what was most noticeable about this silent animal was her air of profound grief. She looked at me out of big brown eyes that were without life and without hope. The confident line I had drawn between animal and human pain faltered and fell away. I had seen this same frightening look in the eyes of abused children and beaten wives; perhaps all victims, be they animal or human, wear this aura of suffering. Convenient plans to dump her on an agency disappeared. This tortured creature needed a sanctuary *now*.

A new beginning calls for a new name. We chose "Kelly." That was the easy part. The difficult part was looking cruelty full in the face. That first week, Kelly crouched under the kitchen table, motionless, silent, her eyes dilated on my every move, refusing to come out except for the times when I literally hauled her outside so that she could relieve herself. She would do her business, then bolt back to her hidey-hole and continue watching me with frightened eyes. I had to place her water and food under the table and leave the room, or she would not touch them. I also had to change my work habits, washing the floor tiles on my hands and knees, because at the sight of my long-handled brush, Kelly's eyes would widen in terror, and she would tremble so violently that her teeth chattered. I knew then what had caused those weals. Any sudden movement or loud noise had her cringing, any attempt to stroke her had her recoiling with little whimperings of fear that brought tears to my eyes. It was a revelation to me. My own father had been a violently cruel man who, after his army discharge, had terrorized my sister and me. I was nine when he began living permanently at home; Cynthia was six. Although damaged by him, I had survived by being able to fight back both verbally and physically; my gentler sibling, however, had gone under. May she forgive my blindness: part of me had always despised Cynthia for her "weakness" in not resisting Dad. But watching Kelly, who had been abused since puppyhood, I realized that it had not been any superior strength of character on my part that had saved me. No, it had been the sheer good fortune of having had an extra three years in which to develop a sense of self; to absorb concepts of justice; to understand that violence is always the fault of the abuser, never the fault of the abused. Those three years had given me a survival advantage that my unlucky sister had never had.

Wanting Kelly to understand that I was not a threat, I began doing my studies at the kitchen table. I believe that animals can sense both aggression and friendship, and so, every day, I would move my legs a little nearer to her. One morning, some six weeks after we had taken her in, I was reading, turning pages with my right hand, my left hand idle on my knee, when I became aware that something small and cool and damp had been placed against my skin, and that it was pressing forward with the utmost delicacy and diffidence. I looked down. Kelly was resting her nose against my hand. She let it remain there, while her expressive eyes looked into mine with a sort of questioning wonder.

Delighted — but moving carefully so as not to frighten her — I praised her and stroked her back where the weals had faded and new hair was growing in. Hesitantly, she accepted my caresses, eventually leaving her sanctuary to stand beside me. For the first time, I saw her tail, a dirty, bedraggled bush, leave its permanent position between her legs and rise tentatively before drooping once more. She leaned against me, looking up at me with simple trust. I knew then that we had won. And when I decided to celebrate by taking her for a walk, Kelly responded with all the joy of a prisoner released from a long and bitter bondage.

Washed and groomed, Kelly proved to be a red-gold beauty. And as her confidence mounted, she revealed characteristics that had been hidden. Although female, she possessed a deep, bass bark: a series of sonic booms that thundered after the mailman, her barking continuing long after he had disappeared. She loved to swim, and would puff endlessly back and forward across the Capilano River, her big red body looking like a rusty tramp steamer. She liked to hide her bones behind the furniture until the whole house hummed with the smell and I would be forced to go on an arduous safari, an anxious Kelly panting at my heels. When I finally tracked down the green, slimy thing, Kelly would snatch it from me, then gnaw it with slobbering gusto, her eyes rolling with bliss. And Kelly shed cloudbursts of red hairs that rained on carpets and furniture and drapes, surged up the rough-cast plaster walls, dammed the vacuum cleaner and floated into the fridge.

She never forgot her early abuse. Whenever I used the long-handled brush, she crawled under the table and became very still, watching me. She was nervous of strangers, and when we had visitors we would shut her in the kitchen, afraid that fear might make her attack. But how she loved us! Her heartbreak when we left her behind while we went shopping; her ecstasy when we returned!

Ten years passed. One day, we noticed that Kelly was having difficulty walking. To our grief, the veterinarian said that she had an inoperable tumour, and it would be a kindness to have her put to sleep. But I couldn't do it; she had become my constant companion. I hoped against hope that the tumour would shrink.

Slowly, Kelly lost the use of her back legs and had difficulty passing urine. No longer did she enjoy my brushing her, and on the last occasion I did so, she yelped and lunged as if to bite my hand. She stopped herself immediately, looking at me with a contrite expression. I knew then that the time had come. We arranged for the veterinarian to come the next day, at one o'clock.

Morning dawned bright and beautiful. The news provided us with yet another example of the terrifying power possessed by some individuals. A dispute about property had broken out between the U.S.A. and Iraq. President Bush was regretful but firm. Television cameras showed him attending church, as if he were briefing Christ, as if he were confident that the Prince of Peace would agree it was acceptable to kill countless innocent men, women and children if America's oil supply were threatened.

Ian and I were enduring our own countdown. All morning, we stroked Kelly where she lay on her blanket in the kitchen, and she responded lovingly, licking feebly at our hands. I couldn't believe, watching that dear, familiar red head, that soon she would be gone from us. In a kind of terrible dream, we watched the hands of the clock move inexorably towards one o'clock.

Dr. Skinner was on time. A kind man, he let us kneel beside Kelly while he arranged his instruments. I cuddled her head and shoulders while Ian cuddled her back legs, ready to control her should she try to bite. But she did not. She was not hostile or afraid, merely puzzled. She stared questioningly at the vet as he first shaved a small area on her paw, then prepared the needle. My heart was pounding; I thought I might choke. Ian was already weeping. When I saw the needle enter, I tightened my arms about Kelly, kissing her soft muzzle and repeating again and again, "We love you, Kelly, we love you." She turned her big brown eyes towards me for the last time, not understanding, but trusting us, and she kept her gaze on me while Dr. Skinner emptied the needle into her vein. She was still looking at me when her breathing changed: it became deeper, slower, and Kelly slipped quietly away from us.

Sometime later, while Coalition generals parried the media's queries about possible numbers of injured and dead in the Gulf, we carried Kelly into the back garden. We had brought her favourite ball with us, on which we had written, "We'll see you again, Kelly. We love you," and we tucked it between her paws, now lying so still upon her blanket. Gently, we lowered her into the grave that Ian had prepared. And then we wept bitterly over this small death.

There is no proof that animals possess souls. But Ian and I are convinced that somewhere, in a spiritual dimension that our science-driven First World has yet to acknowledge, Kelly waits with other beloveds who have gone before us. Kelly is where nobody can ever hurt her again, a place where all power remains with the Creator, not with those who, by their choosing to play God on Earth, have forfeited the right to enter the Heavenly Kingdom.

Ciao, Kelly. Thank you for ten happy years. Thank you for loving us. Thank you for widening my narrow world. A burden? My Kelly, you were a gift.

II: Country Living

Duck for Cover

Phil Butterfield

The first clue that the chimney of our log home was not duck-proof came when, arriving home from a brief spring vacation, we were greeted by feathers and duck poop all over the kitchen and living room. Puzzled and perplexed, we followed a thickening trail of duck detritus downstairs to the basement, ultimately stumbling over the battered remains of a mallard who had been guilty of no greater sin than poor balance or a worse sense of direction. Saddened by the loss of one of nature's feathered creatures, we consoled ourselves that there could not possibly be two such misguided critters in our neck of the woods. How absolutely and totally wrong we were!

Some weeks later I was working in the study when a rustling sound from elsewhere in the house became persistent enough to warrant an investigation. Ignoring our golden retriever, Daisy, lying expectantly at the opening of the fireplace, I searched the house thoroughly without discovering the source of the annoyance. I had not returned to work for more than a couple of minutes when the commotion exploded into a cacophony and the location remained a secret no more. The chimney had been transformed into a battle zone of flapping and squawking that sent Daisy running for cover and me scurrying to the fireplace with a combination of curiosity and trepidation. The trepidation prompted me to pick up a fireplace poker on the way.

Boldly (foolishly, some might say) sticking my head into the fireplace opening, I was greeted by a casserole of soot, feathers and a substance I really don't want to discuss being delivered by a large, orange, webbed foot. This was obviously not a situation for the faint of heart or slow of reaction. On the other hand, I hadn't a clue how to get this misguided migrant off the inner ledge of the chimney it had adopted as a hostel en route to the marsh. Rescue options were definitely limited: the duck could reverse direction and fly thirty feet up the chimney, an unlikely scenario; it could stay put and possibly generate a new subspecies of chimney duck most notable for its singed feathers and black circles around the eyes, an undesirable scenario; or it could come down past the chimney damper and join the party, the most (gulp!) satisfactory scenario. Finally I rounded up a fishing net and a towel, opened the sliding patio door ten feet away and gave the damper one almighty yank. The ensuing seconds saw a large and angry duck showing little respect for the fishing net by charging right through it, and even less respect for its saviour (me) by giving a display of beak swordplay that would make Errol Flynn envious.

Spotting freedom a mere wing flap away, this pterodactyl derivative gave one last arrogant nip to my ankle before nonchalantly waddling through the door and onto the railing of the sun deck. Whether overcome by the excitement of the whole thing or finally reacting to the expenditure of more energy than a raging bull, the duck teetered twice and toppled slowly to the ground. Mustering the last grain of good samaritanism within me, I dashed once more to the aid of the stricken duck, only to see Daisy racing towards it from the other direction at full gallop. As we both came within reach of our quarry, the defiant Daffy gave one barely perceptible hop before taking flight and circling overhead, no doubt chuckling gleefully at the sight of man and dog colliding into a heap of fur and flannel. It's amazing how a little thing like a chimney cap can suddenly become such a big priority in your life.

Avalanche and the Chicken Lady

Deanna Kawatski

One bright spring morning when we were in possession of an old "beater" and an extra ten dollars, and were on our way home from town, my husband and I called on some gentle folk who were living in a teepee. The yard was a clutter of ducks, chickens and geese, and before we left we purchased a rooster that was being persecuted by his brothers.

Crating up the martyr, we placed him and our four-year-old daughter in the broad back seat of the 1969 Chrysler. Smug with self-satisfaction we rattled our way north towards our bush home. Livestock is nearly impossible to obtain in this remote region of British Columbia, and for many months we had been wanting a rooster to keep our hens happy and to enable them to produce offspring.

Upon first perusal the rooster looked like a prime specimen. My husband, who has been a poultry fancier right from childhood, assured me that he should be good breeding stock. The extra large Cornish-Rock was snowy white with scarlet eyes and a comb that wilted slightly under the trauma of transport. On the trip home over the rough gravel road I turned frequently and smiled obsequiously at him, in an attempt to make him relax and feel at ease. I had had a typical small Canadian town upbringing, in which roosters were merely the clay ornaments on the top kitchen shelf, or the proud feathered birds that crowed at dawn from the creaking pages of children's books. I wasn't totally comfortable with the real live things. Little did I know how much, with the passage of time, our rooster's proportions would expand in my imagination.

We called the new bird Avalanche and we soon learned how fitting it was, since he turned out to be a walking disaster area.

He instantly adjusted to his new surroundings, and after putting the flock of ten hens in line he took to strutting and flapping about the chicken yard, the violent beating of his wings resounding like a distant avalanche. When he mated with the hens, as he did methodically ten times a day, always catching them off guard, they'd slide into the dust of the coop as the giant snowball of a bird, in a blizzard of feathers, hit them, full force, from behind.

With only a hint of indignation the hens would rise, shake and compose themselves. The only logical explanation for their acceptance of this abuse was that they didn't know any different. With each fresh assault Avalanche sounded his victory crow from what came to be his favourite pedestal, the top of the compost heap. His crow invariably started off in fine form until he hit the last two notes, at which point his voice would fade out altogether, and any less obstinate neck would have ruptured from the strain that he placed upon it in his attempt to pump out the missing notes. However, this didn't prevent him from delivering his demented bugle call.

His treatment of the hens led to the demise of the most splendid bird of the flock, our daughter Natty's favourite, affectionately dubbed Daffy. Daffy's red feathers gleamed golden in the sun, her comb was bright and as uniform as rickrack, and she was plump and delicious. Avalanche singled her out immediately, and not only did he descend upon her in an avalanche of libido, he also ripped feathers out of her neck in his enthusiasm. The other hens, ever jealous of Daffy because she received most of Nat's attention, welcomed an excuse to pick on her. After Avalanche had cleared a patch at the back of her neck the other hens began to attack the bald spot, and it was downhill from there on for Daffy. She instantly fell to the bottom of the pecking order and was soon the eyesore of the flock, with bald patches and broken feathers. Still, Nat's affection remained fixed on her. We had both spent time with the calm, friendly hens, but under the tyranny of Avalanche they suddenly became aloof.

My first violent confrontation with Avalanche occurred one afternoon when I went into the coop to collect the eggs. The flock was busy scratching in the dirt and I didn't pay much attention to them until I reached into the first nest. I suddenly heard a stampede of feet coming from behind and *whomp*! I yelled as a beak and two feet simultaneously struck my derrière. Avalanche attacked with the force and skill of a karate expert. The three-point strike resulted in a triangle of bruises and an increased reluctance to venture towards the laying nests.

Being petite, I don't like standing beside humans who remind me of this, let alone roosters who make me feel short in stature. Avalanche reduced me to a runt, and I have never felt more like a weasel than when stealing eggs out from under his fierce scrutiny. I tried arming myself with a shovel before entering the coop, but he'd fly over and attack anyway, his beak and feet ringing against it, like a victory gong. He must have sensed that I was afraid of him, and his crimson eyes grew redder and crazier, drunk with power.

As a parent I'm fully aware that it is bad policy to ask your children to do what you yourself are afraid to do, but I found myself asking Nat, in a sugary voice, if she wouldn't like to collect the eggs today.

Avalanche was bigger than Nat, and I loathed myself, as I watched, from the safe side of the fence, while my daughter scurried over to the nests. When Avalanche charged, as he routinely did when a back was turned, Nat held her arms straight out and rushed towards him shouting like a bantam warrior. I watched with amazement as the tyrant turned tail and ran. Natalia calmly went about her business gathering the eggs.

However, the next day when I tried the same tactic, Avalanche didn't retreat. Once again he struck with beak and spur-studded feet.

When I complained to my husband about the unruly rooster his only reply was, "Well, he isn't going to kill you!" Some consolation!

Avalanche waited for his chance to get revenge upon Natty. As she stood in the coop with her back turned one morning the thundering of small fierce feet unexpectedly culminated in a blow to her back that landed her flat on her face in the dirt. Nat didn't cry, but the words that stormed out of her mouth should not have been in the vocabulary of a four-year-old.

Visitors, a couple and their young son and daughter, arrived some time later. It was their first trip to our wilderness home with its idyllic setting. As they stood near the fence and gazed rapturously at the green blush of young wheat and barley in the garden below, and the monarch spruce and towering snow-wreathed mountains beyond, a low rumble sounded from behind. Without warning Avalanche charged the crowd, his feet and beak landing squarely on the back of the small unsuspecting female, knocking her flat. Less stoic than Nat, she wailed loudly, and I experienced outrage. The rotten rooster had made another innocent child bite the dust!

To make matters worse, as the season advanced, at my husband's suggestion, we let Avalanche and his harem have the run of the yard, so that I never knew where he was going to be. He seemed to sense the moment that someone emerged from the house, because he'd strut over with the bearing of a power-crazed general.

So I went on strike. I refused to collect the eggs any more. I dreaded the days when my husband was away because the responsibility fell into my hands again. Eyes red-rimmed from worry, I'd peer from the window to see where Avalanche was before exiting. Or I would listen for the obsessive flapping and crowing to determine his location.

I couldn't admit this concern to my fearless husband. To think that this creature, which I had started out feeling sorry for, now thought that he was lord of all he surveyed, including me. He was making my life miserable.

It didn't help when my husband entered the coop to demonstrate the bird's pluckiness. Arms outstretched, Jay provoked the rooster repeatedly and Avalanche, his eyes and comb scarlet with rage, flew four feet in the air to attack him over and over again. There seemed no limit to his will to kill.

Early one morning in July, when the yard was full of bird song and the smell of wild roses, I quietly opened the door and peeked left, then right. Avalanche was nowhere in sight. I pulled the neck of my full-length housecoat closed against the crisp air. The clear sky held promise of a beautiful day. In one hand I carried the white bucket of yellow "night waters," which we routinely poured over the compost heap to aid in the decomposition of organic matter.

Suddenly out of nowhere appeared Avalanche, first strutting and then charging towards me at top speed, his scarlet eyes indicating a full-blown case of dementia. Alarm clutched my throat, and with the folds of my housecoat flapping around me, I flew to the top of a nearby stump. There I stood helplessly clutching my bucket, while Avalanche, comb flopping beret-style over one eye, and spurs gleaming in the sun that now streamed across the yard, patrolled near the base. I wondered how long I was going to be stranded on the stump and considered shouting for help. Then I remembered that I had but one weapon available. I leered down at the rogue that had bullied me mercilessly all of these weeks and thought, why not? With a single motion I dumped the entire contents of the pail over his feathered finery and instantly doused the flames of his fanaticism.

After that every time I saw Avalanche he showed refreshing respect for me by retreating to some obscure corner of the yard. I noticed that his pace was greatly accelerated if I happened to be carrying a bucket.

Heelers
Don Dickinson

I. Soo

I first saw one in Queensland, Australia, along the rugged grassy hills on the way to the Green Mountains. In the dense heat and among the sawing cicadas, a man in a bush hat and ragged shorts, mounted on horseback, cracked a short whip as he tried to herd a reluctant bull through a corral gate. "Git round 'im, Soo!" the man shouted. *Crack!* "Git round 'im!" The tall grass parted and Soo — stocky, flat-skulled, a mottled gun-metal blue with short-bristled hair like iron filings and pointed ears like a sprinting rabbit's — lunged behind the bull, nipped at the animal's heels, then wheeled away as a slashing rear hoof missed her chops by inches.

"Blue heeler," my Australian hiking companion explained. "Some people claim they're related to dingoes. Could be right. They're good for cattle, but their mouths are too hard for sheep, that's for certain."

The corral gate clicked shut behind the frisking bull. The dog panted alongside the mounted man.

"Good bloody job, Soo," the man said. "Good dog."

II. Pete's Dogs

The Texas Creek Road wanders south out of Lillooet, B.C., and winds along the west bank of the Fraser River with the vague but unconsummated intention of reaching Vancouver. Its first few optimistic miles are paved and painted with yellow lines, but these gradually peter out into gravel, potholes and a washboard surface that climbs hills and skirts rock bluffs and buttonhooks innumerable creeks and gulleys. Dwellings line the Texas Creek Road, huddle next to the mountains or perch on flat benchland overlooking the swirling, muddy Fraser a hundred feet below. Every mile or so one sees a painted corral or a page-wire enclosure or a split-rail fence. Sturdy cabins mingle with suburban-style villas or abandoned shacks. Dust lies everywhere. Viewed from a certain perspective, the Texas Creek Road could be thought to carry a traveller through a hodge-podge of lifestyles and historical times. During the two years that I worked for the local surveyor, the Texas Creek Road took me as far back as Pete Munson's Percheron ranch.

"Pete's a hand-logger," Larry, the surveyor, told me. "He raises the horses to use for skidding logs out of the bush. He also runs a chain saw and drives a logging truck. Pete likes to balance anachronisms."

Larry himself balanced anachronisms. He stowed the latest computerized surveying equipment in a twenty-year-old rusted-out Volkswagen Beetle that jarred and bounced us the twenty-odd miles to Pete's ranch. In the back, doing some balancing of his own, perched Larry's dog, Igor, an eighty-pound off-white malamute. Igor was a quiet, aloof animal whose only real vice was that he liked to kill cats.

"Chase them?" I asked hopefully.

"No, kill them," Larry said. "It's a thing he does. I put it in the Unexplained Genetics category." He glanced somewhat sternly into the rearview mirror. "Isn't that right, Mister Dog — cats?"

Igor's ears drooped and he whined, seemingly chagrined to have his dirty laundry aired in public.

The Volkswagen rattled on, a bucket of nails in a washing machine. It jounced across a narrow bridge and climbed the side hill of a ravine threaded by a single aluminum irrigation pipe. Around a bend, the landscape suddenly opened up into flat green pastureland; thick-necked workhorses gazed dolefully at us from behind weathered corral rails. As we drove up Pete's driveway, a new and intensified racket exploded from the front wheel on the passenger side. *Clackety clackety clackety!* I imagined shrapnel shredding the wheel well, chunks of brake shoes puncturing the hood.

"Wheel bearings?" I shouted.

"Can't be." Larry geared down.

I rolled down the window. An absolutely furious male blue heeler — squat-muscled and spiky-haired — raced alongside the car with his teeth clamped on the front fender like an African hyena trying to bag a gazelle. *Clackety clackety!* He chewed and tore at the metal — dental castanets.

When the car stopped, so did the blue heeler. He stood panting, pressed against his master's leg. Pete, a bearded, shambling man in blue jeans and a pearl-buttoned cowboy shirt, rumpled the dog's ears.

"That's some dog you got there, Pete," I said when we got out.

"He's a caution," Pete allowed.

"Why does he do that?"

"Don't know for sure. Started it a few months back. Friend of mine dropped by in his old Chev, at night. Bucky here herded the Chev into the yard. Bit off a chunk of rusty fender the size of a pie plate. Now he figgers to get lucky, I guess." He thumped the dog fondly. "Had a government guy up here the other day in a brand-new Department of Agriculture vehicle. Bucky tried for the back bumper. Government guy got upset. 'This is a new car!' he tells me. 'I could sue you — lookit the scratches!' I says to him, 'Listen, mister: didn't nobody *order* you to drive into Bucky's yard.'"

Pete stretched. A female blue heeler hobbled down off the porch, snarling in a low, absent-minded way. She was greyer in the muzzle than the male, and her dugs hung low and dark.

"This here's Miss Rebecca," Pete said. "Bucky's mum. She'd probably like to take a run at that car too, but she don't got the teeth for it. Still got the vinegar, though, don't ya, Miss Beck?"

Miss Rebecca grinned.

"See that out there?" Pete pointed. Along the pasture fence something furry ruffled in the breeze.

"Sheep?"

"Nope. Coyote. They got 'im last night. The dog does the chasing, the bitch hunkers down below the fence line. They don't got a chance, them coyotes."

We gazed out over the pasture and considered what did have a chance.

"Am I going to die on this job?" I asked.

Both Larry and Pete chuckled.

Just then half a dozen cats emerged from the barn, sat in the morning sun and preened. Igor, who had stolen out of the car but had drifted into the background like a bachelor uncle, instantly went rigid. His ears and tail dropped; his sharp muzzle found the range of the cats and aimed. He began to slide towards them, one foot in front of the other — a stately, menacing tango.

Snarling, the two blue heelers stiff-leggedly planted themselves between Igor and the cats and bristled like hedgehogs. For a full thirty seconds they stood shoulder to shoulder, guardians of the gates of hell. Igor hesitated, reconsidered. Then with elaborate insouciance he yawned, smacked his lips and wandered back to the Volkswagen to lie down.

"Ah, them heelers," Pete sighed. "Don't nobody mess with their kitties."

III. Angie

According to the woman who owned the farm, the piping little fatty we picked out of the litter was a paradox of breeding, what was known as a "red" blue heeler. Not a purebred, however: a "red" blue heeler-collie cross.

"They make for a gentler mix," the farm lady assured us, as our older son, who was five, gathered the puppy in his arms. The little dog licked his face and sniped at his ears with tiny needle teeth.

On the way home our son dubbed her Angelosha, one of those names that drift out of the ether of a child's mind, like an exotic cloud that has hovered over a bedtime story about Russian peasants and three gold coins and a troll who lives under a waterfall. Of course, within hours "Angelosha" assumed the diminutive "Angie," though in the beginning she retained some Dostoyevskian schizophrenia that in part explained her dual identity. As Angie in the daytime, she frolicked with the kids, gambolled about the yard in buckskin-coloured fur and puppy fat, yipping with delight, tumbling, growling, running off with sticks, rags, shoes. But at night, condemned to a new wicker basket lined with an old sleeping bag out in the porch, she turned inward. Angelosha she became — brooding, morose, warm-nosed, dull-eyed. Every night for two weeks she moped; she lost weight, refused Puppy Chow, paid lip service to saucers of milk. Her sharp upright ears collapsed; her ropelike tail curled between her legs.

"The poor beast is pining," my wife said one night.

I reminded her that we had agreed on an outdoor dog. A don't-pee-on-the-floor, get-up-on-the-furniture or sleep-with-the-kids dog. Tough. Independent.

"Oh, sure," my wife said.

I carried the puppy inside. In what became a nightly ritual, I held Angie in my lap as I read or watched the late-night news. She snuggled against me like a newborn. I fed her dog biscuits with my fingers. She licked my hands, thumped her tail. Later, when the weather grew cold, I brought her basket in and set it beside the wood-burning stove, but she quickly learned to seek comfort at the foot of our elder son's bed. In the mornings, her head lay beside his on the pillow.

"I think Angie loves me," he said once, with such seriousness and awe that the mystery and grace of his observation struck me as profound.

Over the next year Angie grew lean and strong. She constructed, in the manner of dogs, her own mythology. There was the hiking boot she chewed one day in the closet; I wore her teeth marks like a badge ten years after the event. There was the family of bull snakes she killed at the garden wall. There was the down-from-the-mountains bear she chased up the plum tree that night in the fall. There was the day she dragged home a severed leg from some hunter's deer carcass which, an anonymous phone call informed us, had been poisoned. She lay in her basket for three days drooling yellow bile, recovered and never dragged anything home again.

She guarded our children. "Look for Angie," we'd say when the little ones toddled off into the tall grass of the neighbour's orchard. She always lay less than ten feet away from them, ears cocked vigilantly; patient, regal, watchful.

Angie attacked strangers to our yard; never bit, but rushed at them and bunted their legs with her long snout, while red hackles rose along her backbone like rusty wire. Meter readers approached our house warily. Salespeople gave our dog a wide berth. The paper boy poked the *Sun* through the top of the fence; when it rained, the news leaked down the white-painted pickets.

When I jogged she loped not six inches from my heels. If I rode my bicycle, she hugged its rear tire so closely that sometimes her ears flapped in the spokes. On sunny days she lay on her side in the shade of the kids' sandbox while my older son invented stories for her.

We lost her when she was two. On a bicycle ride to a local campground where my wife and children waited for me, I felt the rush of a vehicle behind me, a jolt, a roar of engine and wind as I was flung face first over the handlebars. A pickup truck of partyers whizzed by, the beer drinkers in the truck box hooting in triumph. "All right!" one of them yelled, hammering the truck cab roof. "You got the dog! You got the dog!"

She was dead, of course. Killed instantly, I supposed, although in my confusion and anger I was certain only of the limpness of her still-warm body. "Angie?" I asked her. "Angie?" I carried her gently to the roadside grass, then rode a wobbly mile to the campground where I loaded my bike in the car, returned alone and took her body home.

Later, when I explained to my older son what had happened, he listened intently in the way that children have when they realize they have been admitted into an adult conversation. He nodded with appropriate seriousness, but the rush of grief I expected did not come. Rather, he seemed impressed that his dog had reached this improbable height — death — about which, as a six-year-old, he had speculated little. "Really, Dad?" he said, wide-eyed. "Really? Is Angie really dead?"

"Yes, she is, son."

"Where is she?"

"I put her in the woodshed for now. I'm going up the hill to dig a grave. You can come with me, if you want."

He followed me with his own little shovel, but sometime during the process of clearing away rocks and tree roots, he wandered off. When I had dug the grave, I returned to the woodshed. I had wrapped Angie in a black plastic garbage bag, and my son had freed her from it. He sat on the floor with her head cradled in his lap. He wept silently. "Aw, come on, Angie," he said, rocking back and forth, "wake up. Wake up, Angie."

We no longer live in that particular house. I suppose up the hill from it the grave still stands, a pile of rocks, upon one of which a few dabs of paint might still remain. "Angie. She was my friend" used to be painted there, in a child's clumsy hand. We own a different dog now, a border collie. And a cat, and a mouse, and a hamster. If we mention Angie at all now, it's when one of the younger children stumbles across a photograph in a dusty album. "Who's this?" they might say. "Oh, that's Angie."

But sometimes — on a hike, or in another town, or in the back of someone's pickup truck — a sharp-eared, bristly, gun-metal blue dog will bark, sniff or wag its tail. And one of us will say, "Look, a blue heeler." To which another of us will add, "They're good dogs, aren't they?"

Yes, they are.

Peanut of Metchosin
Gwen Lariviere

My family and I are new residents of Metchosin on Vancouver Island. We love the rural setting, and the sense of comfort and belonging. We did not expect, however, that a tiny creature would give us a welcome we would always remember.

We were strolling down a pleasant country road when we saw a little animal huddled under a tall fir. My husband was sure the thing was alive. When he put it in his pocket for warmth, the tiny bundle started to move. We brought it home. It was about the size of a gerbil. Its eyes were fused shut, like a newborn's. It had a long skinny tail with enough fur to tell us it was a grey squirrel.

I didn't want to be responsible for the life of a little rodent. I was having a challenging enough time giving moral support to my sister, who has bone cancer. A friend advised, "Feed it every three or four hours, 'round the clock. Good luck! You'll need it."

My husband held an eyedropper to the tiny squirrel's mouth. It did its best to suck. "So we let it die?" he asked.

"Let it die?" I thought of my sister, the tubes running into her veins to keep her body as strong as her spirit.

"I'll take the next feeding," I said quietly, as I watched the little creature struggle for life.

We bought a tiny baby animal feeding bottle and filled it with a formula the vet suggested. We laughed as the squirrel sucked on the miniature nipple; how such a little thing could make such obscene smacking sounds was beyond us. We called him Peanut.

Peanut loved to crawl into tight, cosy places. If he wasn't in somebody's pocket or sleeve, he'd be up a pant leg. Once, he got into the crotch of my husband's shorts. Now *there* was ten minutes of hysterics, watching the poor man giggle and grimace as he tried to unhook Peanut's sharp claws from purchase on tender patches of skin.

One morning we looked into Peanut's cage and he was staring back at us. His baby eyes had finally opened. "Didn't expect a family that looked like us," I commented. Peanut scrambled up the side of his cage to get a closer look at his parents.

After that, we discovered where the expression "squirrelly" comes from. Peanut went up his cage and down his cage, sometimes upside-down. When we let him free in the house, he'd scamper towards a doorway, then zip along the baseboard. Back to the doorway! Leap up the doorway! Scrabble on down!

Over long-distance phone, I gave my ailing sister the latest reports on Peanut. As he grew and thrived, her voice became weaker. Her white blood cell count was supposed to be rising. It wasn't, and she was developing life-threatening infections. I would whisper my good-byes and I love you's to my sister, then hang up the phone and go play with my bright-eyed friend.

The day came when my husband felt it was time for Peanut to learn about being a squirrel. Our back deck was where we did most of our outdoor living, but it was twenty feet off the ground. "He's not ready for that yet," my husband decided. We had a fifteen-foot cedar leaning in our living room for a week so that Peanut could learn to climb trees in a controlled environment.

He loved peanuts and sunflower seeds. We loved watching him eat them, perched on his long squirrel toes, tiny fingers holding seeds as his little teeth shredded away at them. But he lusted after peanut butter, and he'd get the goop all over his nose and head.

He loved his bath. He'd let his body go limp in our hands, close his eyes and, with his nose clearing the water, let us gently push him around like a toy boat.

We moved Peanut's cage outdoors. The cage door was left open during the day, and the squirrel was allowed to scamper about the big deck. Sometimes, when he found a patch of sunlight, he'd drop onto his belly, basking in the warm radiance. The times he'd come to a skidding stop at the edge of the deck, just before a twenty-foot plunge, we'd all feel our hearts in our mouths.

One May evening, my sister and I dreamed about the day she'd be released from hospital. We'd sit on the deck, look at the ocean and have chilled Brandy Alexanders while our little friend had peanut coladas. I laughed with her as I hung up the phone, and then I ached inside because her laugh sounded fragile and fading. I walked out to the deck in the quiet of the dusk and looked for Peanut as I prepared to close him in his cage for the night.

I glanced to the right. No movement. I glanced to the left. He wasn't on the woodpile. And then I knew. I walked stiffly to the deck railing and looked down.

I had never realized just how big Peanut had grown in the last six weeks. His tail was almost the length of his body, and it bushed out to look just as round. The soft grass on which he lay was a deep green contrast to his thick grey coat.

When I held him in my arms he was still warm. He looked almost perfect, but I was pretty sure he had broken his neck. I put him in his little cedar home, making sure he had a cache of seeds with him. We buried him under the maple tree at the end of the yard. Everybody cried. I thanked him for being there when I needed him.

A few weeks later the call came from Edmonton. It was my sister. Her strong, clear voice told me her white blood cell counts were up and she'd be coming home, back to Vancouver, soon. I almost cried with relief. All the time Peanut had spent keeping us focussed, keeping us busy with his care and nurturing to save us from the pain of what my sister was going through, all the laughter...

Peanut, I'm sure that Heaven has peanut butter bushes. And I'm sure Metchosin is a little chunk of Heaven.

Accepting Antic
Monica M. Hilborn

All my young life I wanted to be with horses. When I was small I carried a stuffed horse my aunt had given me in my pocket, and later I doodled horses, sculpted them, wrote stories about them and tried in every way that I could to be with them. My parents humoured me, and we would stop on country roads beside fields full of horses so I could see and smell them. Sometimes horses would come near the fence. Frantically, I would grab at the sweet grass and offer it to them, just to keep them close for a little while longer. Their lips would brush my palms and I would stare up into their faces, wondering at the way they watched me as they ate.

Years passed, and adolescence swept me into a world run by hormones and fascination with boys. Then ambition and zeal for knowledge sent me to university to find new friendships, fresh experience and of course more boys, which led to a job, a husband and some stability. I found myself coming full circle and turned once again to horses.

The horse I finally chose as my equine partner was less than perfect according to people who knew a lot more about it than I did. He had been born a twin. The other twin had died, and my horse was the last foal from an ancient mare who had died as he was barely weaned, a history that often makes for a weak horse or one susceptible to disease. He was poorly muscled and had dreadful feet. I saw none of this, of course. I only saw how he floated across the field when he moved, how his golden mane and copper coat would glisten once brushed, and how his brown eyes would watch me when I fed him green apples. His name was Antic.

With great pride and excitement, I brought my new horse into the horse-training community. He was going to be schooled in dressage, where horse and rider execute complex movements in harmony, as if they are dancing. Almost every day I would rush to the barn, my pockets filled with carrots, and groom Antic until not a hair was out of place. On days that I did not ride, I pored over books on dressage or watched the local top competitors ride. Sometimes, while Antic ate, I would stand with my face pressed against the bars of his stall, finding it hard to believe that this radiant creature of cream and gold belonged to me. At last I had the horse of my dreams. I could groom him, feed him and ride him whenever I wished. He was beautiful, and he was mine.

Those were magic days. Every evening spent with my horse was fresh and new. The air smelled sweeter; the cold was never felt; the hours spent grooming and cleaning stalls and tack slipped by. The days became years. The people who had stood around shaking their heads melted away like childhood monsters and were replaced by smiling faces saying, "I always liked him; such a nice horse; knew you could do it." One day I realized that I was no longer the wet-behind-the-ears rider, starry-eyed and just happy to be there, derided by some and humoured by others. Performances at shows and ribbons won had become more than just a fantasy. I no longer went to shows just for fun and experience. I didn't go to the barn just to be with him; it had become part of the process by which I would reach my goals of winning. Muscles rippled beneath my horse's copper-gold coat. His strides ate up the earth. He had become an athlete. And I had become a competitive dressage rider. More than that, I had become engulfed by my ambitions.

One day, at a show, Antic stepped on a nail. This led to an abscess, very painful, said the vet, but not very serious. I nursed my horse carefully until the infection subsided and he seemed as good as new. But before long it became obvious that he wasn't quite his old self. I told myself that he would come around. But it was not to be. Antic became worse and worse until I could not ride him at all. I called in the vets and racked up the bills as we began our search for what was causing him pain. Some days I would be fooled briefly into feeling he was well, but that became part of a painful pattern of ups and downs, ending every time with Antic struggling to move with his old grace despite the agony in his foot.

My vet and I decided to take an extensive series of X-rays to find out once and for all what was wrong. She phoned me with the verdict: severe bone damage in the foot. Together we became clinical as we discussed the options, possible drug and surgical therapies and the expense and success rate of each. Knowing how competitive I was, the vet recommended that I cut my losses and buy another horse. Such a numbness I felt as I hung up the telephone, like cold hands grabbing my shoulders.

For quite a while I walked around like that, my shoulders hunched up around my head and my heart like a rock. I still went to the barn to see my horse every day. I brushed him and cleaned his feet. I brought him apples and stroked his nose. But it was not the same. When I looked at him I no longer saw my diamond honed from the rough, my dream of cream and gold. He was imperfect. He was damaged. No one would want him now. Neither did I.

I began to plan furiously for the future. I had goals to accomplish, and this was not going to stop me. I began to search for a new horse. I wanted to buy the best. I made contacts with breeders and trainers. I talked about what had happened to my horse as a minor setback. I didn't want my fellow competitors to think me foolish for throwing away a riding career on a gimpy horse. I took up running and power-walking for exercise. I had to be busy, couldn't stand still for too long. My dog and I went out for long runs around the neighbourhood, and I would devise dreams about what my new horse would look like, about how successful we would be.

I began to feel that I wasn't running just for exercise but rather to get away from something. My days were filled with a nervous energy, an agitated feeling. One beautiful spring morning I went to visit my poor horse in his paddock. He pricked up his ears and his eyes softened in a friendly, almost playful expression. He lifted his head over the rail and blew warm, clover-scented wind into my palms as he nuzzled for treats. As long as we didn't train he didn't feel the pain and had no knowledge that anything had changed. His innocence blinded him from seeing my betrayal. He didn't know, wouldn't know, until he had been truly abandoned and no one came to see him any more.

I was able to remember something that day. Years before, when I was attending university, my roommate had decided she wanted a cat. We went to the nearest S.P.C.A. on a rainy October night. There was a room filled with cats and kittens in cages, and my friend immediately began to coo over a sweet calico kitten. I left them to become acquainted. In the reception area, a woman in a raincoat with a large, grey tabby cat in a cage walked over to the reception desk, plunking down the cage. "My kids don't take care of this cat any more," she said to the girl behind the desk. "I don't have time to do it. You have to take him off my hands."

I didn't hear much of the rest of the conversation, except the girl trying to convince the woman to keep her pet, since she probably wouldn't be able to find an adoptive home for such a large, older cat. I watched the old tabby as he stared about in confusion. He began to tremble slightly as the voices over him were raised, one pleading, the other strident. All at once, the woman spun on her heel and walked out, leaving the cat on the desk. The girl clucked at the cat sadly, and as she lifted the cage to take him away he began to cry. I ran out and sat on the wet steps, my eyes filled with tears, until my roommate trotted out proudly with her new pet.

As I looked at my horse that crisp spring day, the memory rushed over me and shook my stony walls until they crumbled. I stood with Antic in his paddock and cried, my head pressed against his tall, golden shoulder. I knew then what I had been running from, keeping myself as frantic as a hummingbird so I wouldn't hear what my heart was telling me. I was no better than that woman I had seen years ago.

I phoned my vet that night and told her about the money I had saved, calling it my "new horse fund." But now it was Antic's get-well fund. I told her that I felt I owed my horse every chance to get well. I'm sure I sensed her smile on the other end. She was very willing to switch tactics. We decided to get some input from different vets. The X-rays were sent to a specialist in Saskatchewan. A new drug therapy was embarked upon. Corrective shoes were tried. Money was saved for a surgical procedure if all else failed. My father called in some favours so that I could receive advice from experts in Quebec. My husband, another person who loves me in spite of this "crazy horse business," returned from a business trip, his hands filled with papers he thrust upon me proudly. He had gone to a veterinary college and spent an entire day photocopying every article he could find on diseases of the equine foot and possible cures. I cried that day, too.

I don't think I deserve it, but my horse got well. This spring, my husband skipped out on a baseball game, dragging his friends with him to see our comeback debut at a show. We actually won a class! I feel like I have been holding my breath ever since.

Once again my days are filled with magic. Not because we are competing again, but because I am trying to become a more harmonious, gentle rider. We still go to shows, but now it is for fun. The irony is we are doing better than before. I try to treat each ride like a gift from my horse, not something I have a right to demand. We are making an exchange, he and I, and I have stopped running from my responsibilities.

My mother told me recently that she prayed for Antic almost every day as she does for all members of her family. I think she meant she was praying for his return to health. But I can't help feeling she knew the real loss was that little girl staring in love and wonder at horses through the fence, just happy to be among them. I'm sure the prayer that was answered was that I find my way back there.

Timex

Ken Harris
as told to Denise Anderson

When I lived in Prince Rupert, there was a community ordinance that put restrictions on big dogs. Myself, I didn't feel a huge dog needed to be restricted to the point where it had to be in the yard all the time or on leads when you were out with it. I grew up with a community of people who used their dogs for hunting, trapping and packing, so for me the restrictions that were put on the animals were not correct. My wife and I never had a big dog, but we had two little dogs, a little terrier cross and a miniature poodle: Kissy and Alfie.

Well, I've always had an in for dogs. They're very important. My father used them quite a bit for trapping and hunting. I've known times when a dog will go after a moose and hold it in its place until you walk up to it and kill it with a .22 rifle. For me, dogs are more than just pets, they're really my friends.

When I moved to Kitwanga — that's my home community — for three years after I retired, I had a little three-bedroom trailer, and my family would only come at Christmas and holidays.

I made friends with Timex to begin with. I first learned about Timex when somebody told me that there would be a big dog coming around to my trailer looking for a handout and, sure enough, one day there was this huge Siberian husky, almost a silver-grey with big blue eyes, who stood almost three feet off the ground. He was very friendly, so I went inside and got some food and gave it to him. The next day he was there again at exactly the same time. This is why they called him Timex. I don't know what the original owners called him, but the community called him Timex because he knew when to go to different houses for handouts. Right on time, every time. He was just like a Timex watch. He was very friendly, but so huge that people, if they didn't know him, would be afraid of him.

Timex didn't become a part of my family until one day in the summertime. The grass had grown very tall, and I guess someone was cutting grass with a scythe and left it there. Timex was playing with some children and got his foot slashed. I was home, and I saw these girls coming and I noticed that they were leading Timex and that he was limping. At first, I figured, "Oh, he must have got into a fight," but I couldn't see any dog beating Timex. The children told me, "Timex is hurt." I looked at his paw and saw the skin was just hanging off. Where I had worked before, you had to have some first aid, and I always carried a first-aid kit, so I said, "All right, let me clean up Timex." He was the most gentle dog I ever knew. I cleaned up the wound and then I taped it. Timex just lay down there on the verandah, stayed there, and every day I changed the dressing. It took three or four days for it to heal. Timex never left me after that, and we became very good friends.

I had been to The Pas for one of those trappers' festivals and they used dogs like Timex to pull toboggans, so I thought to myself, "Wouldn't it be nice if Timex could learn something like that." On one of my trips to Smithers, I picked up a harness big enough for him and I got a twelve-foot toboggan. One day I loaded up the toboggan with wood and hooked Timex up to it. As long as you led him, he would pull it. When the original owner noticed that Timex was getting trained, she came over and said, "That's supposed to be my dog." I told her, "Well, I don't know where he came from, but he's been hanging around here." I told the story of how he was injured and how I fixed him and now he wouldn't leave me. The lady missed Timex. It had been about a year and a half — I'd had him all winter. I said, "Sure, have Timex back." I took Timex back to her house and left him there. I had a diesel truck which had a very unique sound, and every time I would go by her house, Timex would pick up the noise and he'd come running with me back to the trailer. Finally the lady said, "I don't think Timex will ever come home again. You can keep him."

Later I had some more dogs with me in Kitwanga — Nisga'a, a wolf-shepherd cross my son picked up, and Private Benjamin, a fox cub a young girl left near my trailer, figuring I would have a soft spot for her.

Taking in Private Benjamin was probably the best thing I ever did. What she did was go after mice in the field. The next thing you know, Nisga'a was doing it and then Timex joined them. Private Benjamin was smaller than the other dogs and always rode in the truck. The other dogs wouldn't go in the truck; they'd always run behind the truck when we went anywhere. We had Kissy and Alfie still in Prince Rupert, and Margaret, my wife, said, "Why don't you take them down to Kitwanga where they can run loose?" So I'd take them down for a week, then take them back to the house in Prince Rupert. Alfie and Kissy were so small I was afraid they might get eaten up by some of the hunting dogs. But before too long I was comfortable with having them there all the time. And the big dogs would look out after the little ones. Anyway, I think between the five dogs, they cleaned up the community of mice.

After three years, I decided to go back to university. I gave the big dogs to my brother. Not long after I left, Private Benjamin was attacked and killed by a pack of dogs. They say that Nisga'a became mean and they were afraid she might hurt one of the young children, so they had to put her down.

Alfie was run over by one of the wheels of my truck by accident, and I left Kissy with my daughter. Timex eventually went back to his natural owner, but he kept up his old routines. When I went back to Kitwanga before coming down to Vancouver, I still had my truck. I said to Margaret, "Watch Timex." As we went by his owner's house, all of a sudden his head went up and he started running in front of the truck back to the trailer. I hadn't been in town for about six months. He was the most beautiful dog. It was the last time I saw him.

A Cow Story

Mariam Habib

This is the story of how one cow changed my life.

During the early 1980s, while working for the federal government, I was going to an important meeting at 100 Mile House. To begin with, the flight from Vancouver to Williams Lake had been delayed. Flustered at this unexpected development in my plans, I was concentrating hard on my driving, very conscious of the fact that the mayor and other community elders would be waiting for me. I was quite oblivious to the beauty of that fall afternoon and the calls of the mallard ducks.

Driving on a dirt road, I had to halt as a herd of cows crossed the road. Impatient at this further delay, I was most annoyed when one cow just refused to budge. She stood right in the middle of the road, staring at me. I shouted at her: "MOVE!" She replied, "Moo." Feeling helpless now, I just sat there, willing the cow to move on. Suddenly I looked into her eyes. Those pools of peace were trying to tell me something, I felt. The message I got was to slow down, to realize that a few minutes would not make that much of a difference.

All of a sudden, the frustration dissolved from my body and I was filled with an overwhelming feeling of peace. I became aware of the balmy October sun, the gorgeous greenery of the countryside, the mallards' cries, the incredible beauty of the Cariboo.

In her own time, my teacher cow, having satisfied herself that I had learned, blinked at me and moved on. I felt sad to see her leave. However, a part of her remains with me. Whenever I feel myself getting overwhelmed with all of life's activities, I think of that glorious afternoon when a cow told me to slow down and take it easy.

Rites of Passage for
My Bunting Billy Goat
Sam Roddan

Many people think a dog is a man's best friend. But what about a billy goat? Nothing united our family more, for a short time at least, than our adopted Billy.

We got Billy when he was two months old, a wobbly little fellow with a bright smile that everyone found irresistible. He flourished on his formula of powdered milk with a dash of sugar and salt. Children loved to take turns feeding him his bottle. The postman and the paper boy stopped by to admire him and tickle him under the chin.

Billy didn't like to sleep in the barn but preferred to sprawl out in front of the TV in the rec room. Sometimes he snoozed for hours on our old chesterfield. I fretted over his behaviour and wondered if this little kid would ever grow up and have horns like more normal billy goats. Then one day I noticed bumps that looked like tiny mushrooms over his eyes. About then I also observed the first traces of adolescent stubbornness, a subtle rebellion, a determination to have his own way.

The arrival of Billy's horns was a source of pride and relief to us all. Now at last we had a real billy goat. And as his horns grew, so did his character and strength of will. Overnight, Billy began to throw his weight around. In no time, he became an expert bunter.

Soon the paper boy, usually as brave as a lion, refused to deliver our paper. The postman complained bitterly. My wife and daughters had their lower extremities severely bruised. Billy chased George, my boy, up a tree. Finally, in desperation, I bought a pair of bicycle handlebar grips and slipped them over Billy's horns. These took some of the sting out of Billy's frolics. But he gradually became incorrigible. Once or twice he bunted the hand that fed him. And that was enough.

After much soul-searching and family discussion, we took Billy to a farm in Cloverdale, a kind of rehab centre for maladjusted animals. The good lady who ran the place said Billy would certainly benefit from down-to-earth therapy. She pointed out two nannies behind a big wire fence frothing at the mouth and barely waiting to get on with the treatment.

From inside the padlocked gate, the nannies stared with ill-concealed delight at their new patient. Billy was startled and taken aback by their formidable presence. Once through the gate he took off, handlebar grips and all, for the safe haven of the barn.

Months later I visited the farm to see how Billy was coping. The change in his personality was unbelievable. Gone were the handlebar grips, and also the old bravado and bluster. As I talked to Billy through the wire fence I noted a quiet confidence, a serenity, a new sense of personal worth and identity. He made no attempt to bunt, instead keeping a watchful and considerate eye on the nannies munching contentedly on the grass beside him.

It was obvious to me that reality therapy had worked on Billy. He had, at last, settled down to become a solid member of the local establishment.

Can a Horse Reason?
Eve MacLean

Kid was a standard-bred gelding owned by Nellie Baker, and he and his rider were familiar figures on the roads around Quesnel.

He was the apple of Nellie's eye. When she strolled into the corral, he would come running to her. "Got a kiss for me this morning, Kid?" she would say, and the velvet lips would nibble gently at her cheek. When Kid was saddled, Nellie would tell him to kneel, and he would drop to his knees, rising smoothly as she settled into the saddle. She rode as though part of him.

Nellie's ranch was about four miles from town along the bank of the Quesnel River, and Kid carried his mistress back and forth, either in the saddle or, when winter came, in the cutter, which he pulled along at a smart trot.

We arrived in Quesnel in the spring of 1915 and moved into a house just off the highway. My husband, Dr. D. R. MacLean, was a veterinary surgeon who soon got to know every horse in the region.

Shortly after our arrival there was an outbreak of equine typhoid in the Cariboo, and a steady stream of horses could be seen coming to our door for treatment and inoculation. As soon as the disease began to spread, Nellie brought Kid to be inoculated.

When the doctor came close enough to use the needle, Kid sensed danger and jumped back, rearing and snorting. Only Nellie's firm grip on the bridle kept him from breaking away. The doctor grasped him firmly and drove the needle home. Kid was furious and fought wildly.

This was the first of many inoculations against typhoid and influenza, and it must have seemed to Kid that every time he came to our place the doctor hurt him. He would snort and edge away even when the doctor only wanted to stroke him. Once or twice Nellie brought him with some minor trouble, to be treated with salve and ointment or massage, and these treatments somewhat allayed his fears.

One autumn morning in September 1919, we were finishing a leisurely breakfast when a neighbour knocked at the door and said excitedly, "Say, Doc, there's a horse out here that looks mighty sick!"

And there, leaning against the verandah rail, not six feet from the door, his head inside — nose almost on the floor — stood the most bruised, battered, scratched and muddy animal I had ever seen. The doctor shouted, "Good Lord, it's Kid!"

His arms around the neck of the horse, one hand feeling for a heartbeat, the doctor murmured, "Poor old boy, whatever have you done to yourself?" Slowly Kid raised his head, looked up with dull, bloodshot eyes, gave a little whinny and laid his chin across the shoulder of his old enemy.

There was scarcely a place on Kid's skin from his nose to his tail that wasn't scraped, scratched or swollen; his mane and tail were bristling with bits of sticks and dried grass, and one hind leg dangled from a dislocated hip. From the faint and uneven heartbeat, the doctor knew the horse was near death.

"I must phone Nellie to come," he said, and handed the broken halter strap to our neighbour. Kid turned his head to watch the doctor, and pulling the strap suddenly, tried to follow. For about thirty feet he staggered, dragging his useless leg in the direction the doctor had taken. Then he gave a long, shuddering groan, and fell.

After Nellie arrived, the doctor performed an autopsy and found Kid had been suffering from a severe attack of enteritis, which causes blinding pain that has been known to send animals mad. Nellie told us that she had heard a noise in the barn in the night, but she thought it was a little mare who had a habit of kicking her stall. She wept unrestrainedly as she talked.

Later that day, Nellie and her stableman followed Kid's tracks into town. It was a trail of struggle and tragedy. The horse had broken his halter strap and kicked his way out of the stall, wrecking most of it, then jumped over the lower half of the barn door. Kid had started off towards Quesnel down the old, unused trail along the river bank. Nellie and her stableman found many places where Kid had been down on the ground thrashing around violently. One part of the old trail was barred off, and the horse had detoured nearly a mile through the woods before coming out on the road again.

Once Kid had fallen over a log, which probably accounted for his dislocated hip. He finally reached the bridge across the river, and from there his wavering, faltering tracks led straight to our door. He had passed without swerving the road leading to the barn where he always stayed while Nellie was in town, where he was fed and sheltered several times a week for years. He usually headed for the barn without hesitation. But it was not the place he wanted this time. What had brought him over this nightmare trail, suffering pain that must have nearly crazed him, to the door of the one person who might have saved his life?

When we were visiting in Quesnel last summer, one old-timer said, "Do you remember the morning Nellie's Kid died on your doorstep? That was the strangest thing I ever saw."

When I told him I was going to write the story, he warned, "Nobody will believe it except the folks who were here."

Nothing in the world will make Nellie believe it was instinct alone that led Kid to our place that morning. Instinctively Kid feared and hated the doctor, would hardly let him put a hand on him, but the fact remains, Kid went to the doctor knowing he needed him.

There have been endless discussions up Quesnel way on the subject. What is the extent of animal instinct? Where is the borderline between instinct and reason? Did Kid really use the latter on that fateful day?

Two Rescues
Rick Favelle

There is much more to being an S.P.C.A. inspector than picking up road kill. Here are a couple of interesting experiences from my years of working with the Vancouver regional branch.

One cold winter day the Surrey shelter received a call that a dog had broken through the thin ice on the Nicomen River. Mike teBoekhorst and I arrived on the scene to discover that the animal was not a dog but a coyote, and that it had been in the frigid waters for five to ten minutes. We discussed which of us was going to venture onto the ice to attempt a rescue; I'm still not sure if it was because I was under Mike's weight or under his seniority, but I was chosen. Fortunately, as I was about to step onto the icy surface, a passerby arrived at the scene with a roof-top boat. In it we moved towards the coyote, catch pole in hand. Our approach was not welcomed, and the animal started to thrash about in an attempt to elude capture. The coyote travelled about five metres before giving in to exhaustion and hypothermia. It started to sink, and I threw the catch pole loop to the fullest extent of my reach. I was able to pull the animal into the boat. The coyote was brought back to the shelter, successfully treated for hypothermia and released.

While in Burnaby I received a call from a distraught young man who said his dogs had been play-fighting and become entangled; the younger dog had the other dog's choke collar caught in its mouth. Upon arrival I encountered a horrific sight. The two dogs were Bouviers, one adult and the other a pup two-thirds grown. The pup had its canine tooth caught in the other dog's collar. The collar was twisted tightly around the pup's jaws, and it screamed in pain. The older dog was frothing at the mouth and appeared to be only semiconscious. As I neared the dogs the pup started to panic and twist all the more. This twisting only added to the pressure on its jaw and the other dog's throat. Adding to the pressure I felt was the fact that the only people at the site were two young teen-aged boys, one of whom owned the dogs.

After finally gaining control of the pup, I needed to determine in which direction the chain was twisted. At this point the other dog had lost consciousness completely, its breathing becoming shallow and sporadic. I was sure it was only moments from death. It took only a few seconds to decide how to unravel the chain, but it seemed like hours. With each twist the pup would yelp and struggle for freedom. Its cries came to an end as I disengaged its tooth. It was only then I noticed that the other dog had stopped breathing. I knelt down beside it, feeling and listening for a heartbeat, but I couldn't find one. I glanced over my shoulder and saw the young man crying and pleading not to let his dog die. I was determined to do what I could, and having just acquired my survival first-aid certificate, I knew I had to try. I cleared the older dog's air paths and started to decompress its chest. I had no expectations, but I couldn't just sit there with that boy only a few steps away. I was contemplating artificial respiration when I saw the dog take a breath. The boy and I looked at each other in near disbelief. I felt for a heartbeat; it was there, faint but gaining strength. Then the paramedics arrived. One went to the vehicle and returned with oxygen for the dog. I then took the dog to the veterinary hospital, where it received a clean bill of health.

Horse in the Well
Linda Wood

The call was clear enough. "We have a horse down a well!" S.P.C.A. Inspector Linda Wood thought she was hearing things.

The dispatcher was insistent. "Drop whatever you're doing and respond, please!"

Linda took the address and started driving, but her thoughts were grim. What awaited her? Would she find a prize-winning thoroughbred wedged grotesquely upside-down? A child's pony drowning on its back? Hysterical women and children? It had been grey and damp all day. As night approached, the roads were becoming more and more slippery. She found herself driving faster and faster.

On her arrival at the scene, Linda found only a lonely farmer standing in a pasture between his house and the barn. Within seconds, two other S.P.C.A. inspectors, Mike and Kim, appeared, as well as several neighbours. As they all gathered dumbfounded around the well, an uneasy silence enveloped them.

There was the horse six feet below, sitting squarely on its haunches, back vertical with the well wall, water up to its elbows.

Suddenly, the chatter resumed, and everyone had a different suggestion.

"Get ropes!"

"Call the police!"

"Bring my truck up!"

"Find a gun!"

For a moment, shooting the poor horse seemed like the most merciful thing to do, rather than putting it through the trauma of an impossible rescue. Fortunately, the cooler heads of the S.P.C.A. prevailed. The horse seemed calm, but the owner had no idea how long it had been stuck there. Was it injured? Was it in shock? Linda called for a veterinarian and a tow truck, then retrieved the livestock sling from the back of her van.

Mike and Kim lay flat on the grass, peering over the edge of the well. Fearing that the horse might start thrashing its head against the cement casing, they inched forward as far as they dared and slipped two ropes through its halter. Getting the sling around its body would not be so easy. Mike and Kim slipped a rope around each front hoof, and as they coaxed and pulled that soggy, unyielding body, onlookers lowered Linda by her ankles over the edge to slip the sling around the horse's barrel.

For what felt like an hour, Linda tried to find a crack between the horse and its prison wall. But nothing was working. Just when the moment seemed right to slide the sling into place, the horse flung its head towards her. She twisted her body to avoid the collision, but their heads met. Dazed and frustrated, Linda was pulled back onto the wet grass.

Mike had an idea. "Let's call the fire department."

What had once been a quiet moment between a farmer and his estranged horse soon became a full-blown spectacle. Red, orange, white and blue lights spun and flashed against wet and weary faces. The headlights from S.P.C.A. vans, fire trucks, police cars and the tow truck now illuminated the busy scene around the well.

After some conferring, it was decided that if the water level was lowered in the well, it might be easier to coax the horse to accept the sling. Dr. Galmut, the vet, volunteered to be sling operator, but this time the firemen strapped him into a harness. Slowly, the hose, the vet and the sling descended. The hose dipped into the water, and the order was given to start the pump.

No one breathed. To their horror and dismay, as the water level dropped, so did the horse, deeper and deeper into what seemed destined to be its grave. Dr. Galmut had no desire to follow and motioned to be pulled up. The pump was stopped. The horse was now *sixteen* feet down the well!

What next? Each person looked helplessly but hopefully at their neighbour, silently praying for a miracle.

"Why don't you put the water back in?" a small voice said.

Linda caught Mike's eye; Mike turned to Kim; Kim looked at Dr. Galmut; all three turned to the firemen. They had all heard it. What did they have to lose?

"Okay. Turn the water on!"

Inch by inch the water rose. For a few seconds, the horse didn't move. Then, inch by inch, the horse rose too — inch by inch until the well overflowed, and the horse climbed out. It started eating grass immediately, and everyone laughed and cheered.

Linda wondered for years afterward who belonged to that small wise voice.

Poopen the Cat
Marilyn Piters

Our daughter, Heidi, adopted Poopen fifteen years ago when he was a kitten. He became her companion, confidant and true friend, loving her unconditionally. He survived being hit by cars three times, earning him the nickname "Speed Bump." Heidi moved her household several times over the years, and Poopen accepted each move philosophically and adjusted well.

When Heidi acquired two dogs, Chinese chows, Poopen decided it was his responsibility to bury their droppings. Not too big a chore, since Poopen was a strong, muscular cat. It was not unusual to look out the window and see Poopen hard at work burying the dogs' waste.

All went well until the entire family moved to a forty-acre farm. The farm is home to eight horses. The look on Poopen's face when he saw the size of those "horse pies" was heartrending. The poor cat felt he had to conceal the horse apples. We would sadly watch Poopen, elderly now, trudge up the driveway in the morning on his way to work. I felt like giving him a tiny lunch pail! He would work all day out in the pastures and paddocks, burying horse droppings. He would drag himself home in the evening, weary and sore. We tried to stop him, to spare the old gent this back-breaking labour, but he would have none of it. Off to work he would go each day.

He is thin now and sleeps a lot. He doesn't go to work any more. He has retired. He eats well, purrs when petted and loves to snuggle into a welcoming lap. But we know he won't be with us long. The whole family visits him and gives him lots of affection in these last few weeks of his life. It's rather like visiting an elderly and beloved grandfather in a nursing home.

There will be an empty space in our family when Poopen leaves us. Our comfort will be that he had a wonderful cat life, surrounded by a family who loved him. When the time comes, we will bury him on our farm...far away from those dreaded horse pies.

Still Life with Animals
Sandy Frances Duncan

When I bought my house on Gabriola six years ago I was charmed by the deer that wandered out of the adjacent forest and browsed their way across my lot through sword ferns, long grass and salmonberry. The house had been rented to people obviously not interested in gardening; a few deer-trimmed calendula struggled in a raised brick planter along the side of the house and the grass had not been mowed in years. I wasn't interested in gardening either, I thought, but house-warming gifts materialized as roses, rhododendrons, azaleas and spirea. I hooked yards of plastic fishnet over the planter and on other plants hung deer-retardant soap or hair collected from the hairdresser in bags made from old pantyhose. The deer left those plants alone, at least until the rain washed the smell away. (The rain washed one of the bags away, too. I found it later in the spring when it wrapped itself around the lawnmower blade, to the demise, in blue smoke, of the engine.)

For a few years the deer and I coexisted on different sides of the increasing yards of plastic fishnet as my gardening enthusiasm grew. I didn't bother fencing the rhododendrons; the book listed them as "deer-proof plants." Unfortunately, Gabriola deer have not read this book.

Finally the deer figured out how to lift off the fishnet, eat the plant it was protecting and replace it. I ordered up a fence. Seven feet high, the top two feet cantilevered out at forty-five degrees: deer won't jump something protruding over their heads. (So far, it seems that they *have* read this book. Forgetting to close the gates, well, that's my problem.) But I only fenced a portion of my lot — half for me and half for them, I said as I rolled up the yards of plastic fishnet. All winter I dug new flower beds.

With my gardening enthusiasm now in full bloom, I faced another problem. The Gulf Islands have a Mediterranean-type climate: no rain. At least, not in the summer. I ordered up the cheapest cistern, an above-ground swimming pool, three feet high by fifteen in diameter, capacity 2,700 gallons, fed by extensive aquaducting off the house and carport roofs. Then kindly friends informed me that I had created an enormous breeding ground for mosquitoes and I needed fish to eat the larvae.

So I went to the pet store and bought thirty small goldfish, a dozen for five dollars — they're called feeder fish and I didn't want to inquire why — and plunked them in the cistern, after the requisite half-hour to equalize the temperature of the water to their plastic bag. Then I needed to buy fish food, because this was April and there weren't any mosquito larvae yet. Then I needed to buy water plants so the fish could hide if a heron or kingfisher passed over. By now, I couldn't call the swimming pool a *cistern*, I had to call it a *pond*.

I kept the fish food in a plastic bag on a high ledge of the carport next to the pond; one morning it was missing. I found the empty bag weeks later near the raccoon tunnel through the salal. I should have known. This same raccoon had opened the cupboard on my back deck, pulled out the birdseed and invited every bird to the party. But they didn't finish the leftovers; within six weeks I was weeding the cracks of my deck. And I suspect that this raccoon stole my brand-new leather gardening gloves, for which I will never forgive it. I moved the fish food to a coffee tin.

I have a friend who has named the fish in her pond. She has Spot and Flash and Tail, etc. I couldn't name my fish because I was too busy counting them. Thirty, twenty-nine, twenty-seven, twenty-three — by the following spring, twenty had survived. Statistically correct, according to another friend who had told me to expect to lose one-third.

We had an unusual cold snap my first fall with the fish, and ice formed on the pond, six inches thick. I found myself trying to peer through the ice and panting. *Poor fish, can't get to the surface, can't breathe!* I panted harder, then sternly told myself that I was overidentifying.

After a rain storm that winter or spring, I noticed a fish lying on the ground by the overflow drain. It had obviously been washed down the four feet of corrugated plastic pipe. I didn't know how long it had been out of water, but it was undoubtedly dead. I wandered off to get the shovel and ended up doing other things. It was half an hour before my return. When I stuck the shovel under the fish, it flipped over and wriggled. Surprised, but convinced its death was imminent, I shovelled it into a pail of water. Two days later, the fish hadn't yet died, but it was languishing — not swimming, not eating. Clumps of mud still clung to its scales. I hadn't brushed them off for fear of hurting the fish; besides, it was going to die. Thinking it might as well expire in familiar surroundings, I dumped the contents of the pail into the pool. The fish paused, then flicked its tail and took off. The other fish swam over, seeming to greet it. *There you are, where've you been?* And the overflow fish looked as if it were saying, *Where've I been? You really want to know? What a story I've got to tell!*

Then the fish started fighting — or that's what I thought. They would gang up on one poor soul and chase it around and around, with much splashing and excited ruckus. At first I tried to rescue the victim from its hiding place in the reeds, but then I realized the fish were spawning, and

being as noisy about it in their own way as cats or humans. I felt rather
foolish. For months, one or two mornings a week I'd look out the
window and see the surface of the pool roiled in erotic frenzy. I felt a tad
embarrassed and found myself wanting to stay away until the water was
calm again.

One day I noticed one of the goldest fish now looked like a miniature
airplane: it had grown ominous long white furry wings on either side. I
readied the hospital pail and scooped the fish into it. While I was
debating whether to phone the Nanaimo S.P.C.A. or the Biological
Research Station, a friend told me that she had a friend who was a
veterinarian with a specialty in fish. I phoned for a consultation. "Highly
contagious. Good thing you isolated it. Scrape the fungus off with a
spoon and apply tincture of iodine, diluted four to one."

Stifling my squeamishness, I procured the iodine and swabs for applica-
tion, found an old spoon I had used for cat food before my catless period,
readied a sheet of plastic and pulled on my latex gloves. I hadn't asked if
the long white fuzzy fungus was highly contagious to humans. I scooped
the fish out of the pail, scraped, fighting nausea, and applied the iodine.
The fish lay quietly, good as gold. I told it so as I returned it to the pail.

Within days the fungus grew back. I repeated the treatment. I
explained the problem to everyone I knew, including the pharmacist. He
dragged out a tome of pharmacopoeia that recommended an incremental
saline solution. I procured high-grade sea salt and started dumping it in.
The fish spent its time, between scraping and iodine treatments, gasping
at the surface of the water.

I remembered how the overflow fish's languor in the hospital pail had
seemed related to social deprivation — after all, fish hang out in
schools — and I felt sorry for the fungal fish's enforced solitude. By now
it had valiantly spent ten days being treated. The only happy entity was
the fungus. After more consultation and soul-searching, I committed
euthanasia with the blunt end of the ax. Then I vomited.

The next time I had a fish patient I didn't do anything but read a
library book. It told me that my asymmetrical fish probably suffered
stuck spawn and the treatment was external massage and internal ream-
ing out. This was beyond me. Besides, she swam happily about, ate and
interacted with her peers, growing all the time more asymmetrical. Last
week, I found her floating, three months after my initial diagnosis.

I would like to think that the rest of the fish, uncountable now with all their babies, consider the pond fish paradise. They have reeds, water lilies, iris and floating hearts to swim around; water skaters, water boatmen and snails for interspecies variety; dragonflies, Stellar's jays, bandtail pigeons, wasps and the neighbourhood cats for above-surface visitors. And they don't have my problem: I can't water the garden because it might deprive the fish.

Lum King's Horse
Norma Charles

It was a sunny Monday morning in the spring of 1949, and that meant one thing at our house: Washing Day. In those days before automatic washers and dryers, when everything from shirts to pillowcases was starched and ironed, Washing Day was a whole day's work, and every member of the family helped. My job was entertaining my little brother to keep him out of the way.

I was reading him a story under the kitchen table when there was a rap on the door. It was Lum King, our Chinese neighbour, who had a huge vegetable garden across the lane from our house.

"Ah, Lona." That's what he called me. "New spring vegetables for the family," he said, handing me a burlap bag.

"Thanks," I said, nodding my head to him.

Right behind him, nodding her head as if she were mimicking me, was Lum King's horse. She had followed him right up to our door. She followed him everywhere with the devotion of a faithful old dog.

"How's your horse?" I asked, patting the old horse's velvety nose.

"Horse? Ah, horse. Good, good." Lum King nodded to me and left, his horse clopping right behind him.

When I got back to the table, I found my little brother curled around the book, fast asleep. My mother said to cover him up and yes, I could go out for a while, but not for too long because she would need me again soon. I got a couple of sugar cubes and headed out.

Yellow-green sunlight filtered through the new leaves in our back-yard. I took a deep breath of the cool spring air. The long grass was sprinkled with hundreds of white button daisies. Perfect for a daisy chain. Soon I had gathered a whole skirtful of tiny flowers.

I wandered across the back lane to a sunny spot on a high grassy mound to make the chain. From my perch I could overlook Lum King's farm and his tarpaper shack, which squatted like a friendly bear at the edge of his huge vegetable garden, straight rows of lettuce and beans, carrots and tomatoes.

We had recently moved to B.C. from Manitoba and I hadn't met many kids yet, so Lum King was probably my best friend then. Not a bike-riding or baseball-playing kind of friend, but the kind of friend you were comfortable with without even trying. Whenever I was lonely and miss-ing my old friends, I could always console myself that at least Lum King thought I was someone special. He let me help in his garden, pulling weeds and collecting plump red radishes and long thin spring onions. That spring he had given me some cucumber seeds to plant on a sunny square of rich brown soil between the back lane and his own rows of spring vegetables.

I stood up to try to spot Lum King. There was no sign of his straw-hatted head bent over the rows of new plants. He and his horse must have gone up to the store. Or maybe he was in his house. I would wait on my mound for them and finish my daisy chain.

I had never seen anyone but Lum King go inside that tarpaper shack. He didn't seem to have any relatives. And the horse was his only friend besides me that I knew of.

After a while he emerged from his shack. He always looked the same, as if he had grown out of the brown soil of his garden. His wrinkled brown face blended with his dusty work clothes.

"Ah, Lona. Look at new cucumbers yet today?"

"Not yet. Where's your horse?"

"Horse? Ah, horse." As if in answer to being called, Lum King's old mare came out of a lean-to attached to the shack. She nudged Lum King's shoulder. He rubbed her nose gently, clicking a soft message into her ear.

The horse had probably once been a great help in his garden, but now she wasn't any help at all that I could see. She was going blind and deaf.

Although Lum King never rode her, her back swayed into a deep U. He had even stopped putting small loads on her back. He carried the loads himself, slung over his own broad shoulders. The only thing the old horse could do was follow him around. Whether Lum King was weeding the long rows of vegetables, or walking up to Young's market store on Blue Mountain Road, there was the ancient mare, clip-clopping along right behind him, her nose nudging his shoulder.

I wandered down to pat the horse and offer her a sugar cube, which she lapped up with her long, grey, sandpaper tongue. Lum King ducked back into his hut. I rubbed the mare's warm neck and she lowered her head so I could reach between her ears. As I scratched her forehead, her long-lashed eyelids fluttered shut and she sighed.

Soon Lum King returned with a generous piece of butter cake still warm from his oven.

"You eat. Good," he said, offering it to me with cupped hands.

The cake was as rich and golden as that spring day. The horse sniffed loudly and neighed a begging chuckle.

"Ah. So you want cake too." Lum King disappeared into his hut again and returned with another large slice. He grinned when it vanished with one flick of that sandpaper tongue.

I brushed the horse's speckled brown coat hard with a stiff wooden-backed brush. But no matter how much I brushed, I could not get it to shine.

The horse wrinkled up her skin, snorted softly down through her nose and nodded her head. She loved being brushed.

Lum King filled two large gunnysacks with fresh spring vegetables — lettuce, onions, radishes. Then he slung the sacks over his shoulder.

"Going up to Young's market to sell these good springtime vegetables," he said. He smiled his round-toothed, wrinkle-eyed smile and headed down the gravel lane.

I gave the horse one last pat on the rump, then she clippity-clopped away to follow him. When Lum King came to the end of the lane, he turned right, which meant he was taking the long, roundabout route to the market. That way he would avoid the hard pavement and also the kids' cruel taunts of "Chinky, chinky chinaman." My face burned at the thought of those dumb kids yelling whenever they saw him. He would raise his head proudly and stare straight ahead, ignoring them. After a while, they would get bored and leave.

I climbed back to my grassy mound and soon finished my daisy chain. I hung it in a loop on Lum King's door handle. Then I meandered past the clover field that Lum King's horse often shared with baseball-playing kids. There was no game that day, so I wandered on to the ravine.

The ravine was a place that looked as if a giant had slashed a huge gouge out of the land, leaving a swift bubbling stream at the bottom and steep cliffs on either side that were covered with prickly blackberry bushes and tall cedars. My older brother said it was not a giant knife that had cut out this ravine; I knew that, really. He said it had been carved all right, but by the stream that flowed at the bottom. The only time you could believe this theory was in the spring, when the stream swelled up like a real river with the heavy rains and melting snow.

My brother and his friends had tied a long rope to one of the high branches of an especially tall cedar tree that overhung the crashing stream. I shimmied up the tree to a broad branch worn shiny as glass by many other climbers. After swaying around in the breeze for a while, I grabbed the end of the rope and slithered down.

I carried the rope up the bank as far as I dared. Hanging onto the thick knot, I wrapped my legs around the rope. Then I took a deep breath and leapt out over the ravine. Down towards the splashing stream I dipped, leaving my stomach behind.

The rope tightened. Up the opposite bank I glided. For an instant I hung high above the bushes, then down towards the stream I swung again. Then back up, up the steep cliff. And down. What a glorious sensation!

After a few more swings, the jumps became too tame. Dragging the rope, I climbed to a higher ledge. I had never dared leap from such a high place before. But other kids had done it, so why couldn't I?

I twirled one leg around the rope and grabbed the knot tightly, so tightly my knuckles stood out white against my tanned hands. I inhaled deeply and squeezed my eyes shut. Then I leapt.

Falling, falling, falling, I almost touched the stream. The rope yanked tight and I drifted halfway up the other bank, bushes clawing my legs. Then back down again I swung. Suddenly, the rope snapped!

I gasped and plunged into that bubbling cascade. The frigid current grabbed me. Down it towed me, flipping me over in the crashing water like a helpless pebble in a rock tumbler. Frantically I flailed about for something to grab — anything. Nothing was solid. The world was flashing water. Grey, black, brown. Which way was up? Panic seized me. I could not breathe. My lungs were bursting! I gulped water, gallons of it.

Darkness descended. Then a crashing silence. Drowning. I was drowning.

Suddenly my hair was caught. Now my tangled hair was dragging me down. I thrashed about wildly to escape.

"It okay, Lona. It okay." Lum King! It was Lum King! My friend was tugging me out of that violent water.

I grabbed at his shirt, his firm, steady arm.

"It okay. It okay," he murmured calmly, soothingly. He drew me out of the torrent. I huddled at the muddy edge of the stream, coughing up water, gasping, struggling to breathe. As he waited for me to catch my breath, he seemed uneasy, apprehensive. He kept staring up at the steep bank.

While he was helping me over some prickly blackberry bushes, there was a loud crash directly above. Something huge was plunging down the bank towards us. Instinctively I flung myself down and buried my head under my arms.

I heard Lum King utter a low guttural cry. He leapt forward.

Then I saw her! His horse! Lum King's faithful horse! His dear half-blind, almost deaf old mare! She had tried to follow him as usual, and had lost her footing on the slippery bank above.

She screamed as she struck the stream head first. The swift waters swept the old horse under and dragged her downstream. The torrent propelled her against a boulder in midstream, her rump sticking grotesquely out of the water, her head thrust deep into the rushing stream.

Lum King lunged through the dense undergrowth towards his horse. He stumbled and sprawled into the bushes. A root had caught his foot. Frantically, he worked himself free. Then he scrambled through the thorny bush on his knees, uttering words in some language I could not understand.

He knelt at the edge of the stream, his bleeding face contorted in anguish. Tears washed down his leathery cheeks. He swayed back and forth, hugging his knees. He moaned and he moaned.

I heard another man's voice.

"What's going on down there? Do you need help?"

"Help!" I managed to croak. "Oh, please help us!"

It was Mr. McFarlin, who lived near the ravine. He clambered down the steep bank. He stared at my soaked clothes, pulled off his flannel shirt and thrust it at me.

I clutched it and whimpered through chattering teeth. "Lum King! Over there! Help him! His horse!"

Mr. McFarlin scrambled to where Lum King huddled by the water, staring at his overturned horse. Mr. McFarlin talked and Lum King shook his head. He would not move. He would not leave his faithful old companion.

Mr. McFarlin helped me up the bank and took me home. My mother dropped her ironing and stuck me into the laundry tub in the middle of the kitchen before she even let me explain what had happened. It took a long time in that sudsy water for my teeth to stop chattering.

My father and older brother, who were building a shed in the backyard, dropped their tools and raced down the ravine with Mr. McFarlin. My brother told me later that there was not much they could do. They tugged the drowned horse out of the water with ropes. Then they assisted Lum King, who had wrenched his ankle, up the bank.

The next day all the neighbours helped Lum King bury his horse in the clover field by the ravine. He placed that long daisy chain I had made on top of the dirt mound. After that, we always called that field Lum King's horse's field.

Lum King seemed to grow older and more stooped overnight. Now he walked with a limpy shuffle, supporting himself with a cane. But always alone. Now he had no faithful old mare to keep him company.

One thing though, kids stopped taunting him, even when he walked straight up the sidewalk to the store with his sack of vegetables slung over his shoulder.

I even saw some of those kids stop and talk to him sometimes.

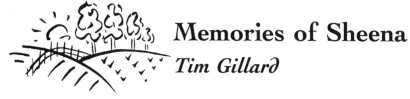

Memories of Sheena
Tim Gillard

It was 4:30 A.M. I reached over to turn off the alarm before it went off. Sheena must have heard me get up because she came into the bedroom all excited. The night before she had watched me getting my camera, rifle and pack ready. So she knew we were going somewhere. Sheena was my four-year-old, long-haired German shepherd. Best friend and loyal companion, she went everywhere with me.

The weather forecast was for mixed sun and clouds with a chance of flurries and −15° F. I had had this day trip planned for a long time. We were headed into a remote valley near Pine River. It was about an hour's drive from Fort St. John, the northern B.C. city where I lived, to the spot where I planned to park my truck. We were going there to take pictures and scout for the upcoming elk and deer seasons. There were a lot of black bears and even the occasional grizzly in the area. I was going to take my .303 rifle with me just in case. Having Sheena along always made me feel better when we were in bear country.

Sheena loved riding in the truck. She would sit in the passenger's seat and push her nose against the windows, putting nose prints all over them. An hour later we got to the old oilfield road that would take us closer to the valley. The snow was deep on the road and was almost pushing over the hood of the truck. We saw a group of deer in the field beside the road just as it started to get light. Sheena noticed them first; the side window was up but she saw their silhouettes. I stopped and slowly rolled down the window to get a better look. There were two four-point bucks, two spike bucks and ten does, all whitetails, about twenty yards away. At first, Sheena just sat there, tail wagging, and growled slightly. The deer stood perfectly still, until Sheena barked. What a beautiful sight: four bucks and ten does, all with bright white tails flashing, bouncing stiff-legged, single file through the deep snow with the sunrise in the background. It reminded me why I had gotten up so early on my only day off in two weeks. About five miles down the road we stopped and parked. I had no sooner let Sheena out when she took off barking towards the trees. Luckily the porcupine had seen us first and had made it up a tree before Sheena got there. The sun was coming up, so after a few pictures we headed towards the valley.

There was a hard-packed game trail with a fresh set of coyote tracks heading straight down the hill. Sheena walked ahead of me, constantly looking back. We walked about an hour before stopping to take some pictures of three ruffed grouse sitting in a tree. The trail was quite rough; there were a lot of fallen trees across it and the willows were very thick in places. You could see the whole valley from certain spots. I noticed a doe standing on the crest of a hill ahead. Sheena was ahead of me and hadn't even noticed it yet. That was strange, because she almost always noticed animals first. She seemed nervous, sniffing the ground and then backing up towards me. Then I saw why: there was a fresh set of bear tracks heading straight down the trail we were on. The tracks were huge. I wondered if it was a black bear or a grizzly. I stopped and put Sheena on her leash and put a clip of shells into my rifle. Not much farther along we saw a beautiful young bull moose. The bear was staying mostly on the trail but kept veering off into the bush. Sheena was intently sniffing the trail and even whining at times, so I knew the bear couldn't be very far ahead. We were both startled by a red-headed woodpecker banging away on a tall birch tree. The bear tracks had disappeared into the trees. About nine o'clock we spotted the bear about five hundred yards ahead of us on the trail. We kept following him for a while.

We lost sight of the bear and stopped for a bite to eat. Milkbones for Sheena and sandwiches and cookies for me. I figured we were about six miles from the truck. Before we got up, I used my scope to look back down the trail. The bear had circled back and was coming up the trail behind us. I decided to stay out in front of him. I put Sheena back on the leash and kept going.

My rifle, across my back on a leather sling, was starting to make my neck sore. So I pulled it forward and walked with my right hand on the barrel of the gun, the rifle horizontal to my shoulder. My other hand on Sheena's leash.

We came to a big birch tree that had fallen across the trail. I boosted Sheena over, then climbed up onto the log, still holding the gun barrel and Sheena's leash. Before I could jump down, I slipped, falling backwards.

The gun's scope caught my head right near the ear with tremendous force. All I remember is a massive surge of pain and seeing a bright flash of stars.

I woke up to Sheena licking my face and pawing me. My head hurt really badly, and I was very cold, weak and dizzy. I realized I must have been unconscious for some time. I had blood all over me, enough to soak the front of my T-shirt, sweatshirt, lumberjack shirt, jeans, long underwear and even the sock inside my left boot. Every time I moved my head, the gash, which felt about three inches long and very deep, would start bleeding again. I took my T-shirt off and wrapped it around my head for a bandage. I was shivering very badly.

It was going to be getting dark soon, and it was at least four hours' walk back. We started walking but could only make it about fifty yards before I had to stop. I was tired and out of breath; losing so much blood had made me very weak. I could feel blood running down my neck. My head hurt terribly as I sat down holding onto Sheena. She noticed something. I looked up to see the same black bear from earlier, standing back at the log where I had fallen. I got my gun off my shoulder and loaded a bullet into the chamber. Sheena was growling, and the hair on her back was standing straight up. I was shivering so much I wasn't sure if I would be able to shoot if the bear did attack. But he walked off the trail into the bush. We got up and started walking again. Soon I had to stop again. Sheena, by pulling on the leash with my encouragement, had been helping a lot. She was also keeping me warm when we stopped. After resting a few minutes I got up. Just then we heard crunching in the bushes very close to us. Sheena was barking and I was starting to get really scared. It was the bear. I could smell him. I fired a warning shot into the air, then loaded the gun again. We started walking as fast as I could. It was starting to get dark, and I was getting weaker and weaker. After another mile without hearing or seeing the bear, we stopped to rest again.

The next thing I knew, I woke up with Sheena whining and licking me on the face. I wasn't sure how long I'd been asleep, but it was dark now and I was very cold. I got out my flashlight, and we started out again. I was dizzy and very thirsty. My head was still bleeding off and on. The bear was still around. His tracks were on the trail again.

I figured it must be at least eight o'clock. I was shivering constantly now. We stopped to rest again. Even though I kept telling myself to stay awake, I couldn't. Sheena woke me up again by pawing at me. We were getting closer to the truck now. The trail got rougher and steeper as we climbed out of the valley. We heard an owl hooting at the moon. I was getting worse and worse, so tired and cold. I remember praying for God to help us get back to my truck. I kept telling myself I'd be okay if I could just get there. The batteries in my flashlight were fading. Somehow that seemed funny to me, and I started laughing. I was starting to get hypothermia. I remember thinking, what would someone think if they saw me coming down the trail, blood all over me, laughing my head off? The next time I stopped Sheena had to wake me up again. I was scared that one of these times I would freeze to death.

We could hear coyotes howling in the distance. After a few more rests and one last hill that seemed to take hours to climb, we made it to the truck. I can't remember ever being so happy to see a vehicle. Sheena was happy too, running around barking and jumping up at the door. I will never forget the sound of the motor starting. I was going to make it! I turned the heat on full blast and we were off.

The next thing I remember is Sheena pawing at me again. I had fallen asleep at the wheel and hit the ditch. My chest hurt. I hadn't put my seatbelt on, and I must have hit the steering wheel on impact. I had taken the bandage off my head when we got into the truck. The crash had split the wound open again, and there was a puddle of blood on the floor. I remember holding onto Sheena and crying. I could hardly stay awake, I had no strength and I was dying of thirst. I got out into waist-deep snow to try and lock the hubs into four-wheel drive. The ditch was steep, and I wasn't sure if I would be able to get out. My heart was racing as if it was going to explode. After four tries, I was back on the road again. We were only minutes away from the Alaska Highway now. After almost falling asleep again, and nearly hitting the ditch, we made it onto the highway.

There wasn't a car or truck in sight and I couldn't see any lights even off in the distance. I parked my truck across the highway with the flashers on. I wanted to make sure someone would find us if they came along. It must have been about three or four in the morning. There was no way I could drive myself into town; I was too tired. My head was still bleeding off and on, and my chest really hurt. The last thing I remember is hugging and talking to Sheena.

All of a sudden I felt someone shaking my arm. I woke up, startled, and sat up. I was in Fort St. John General Hospital. Some people had come along, found me unconscious and brought me into town. The first thing I said was, "Where is Sheena?" The nurse told me she was in the waiting room. I had been out for about four hours. The doctor had stitched me up and had given me blood and fluids. It was morning now, and I wanted to see Sheena. She had saved my life, and I wanted to thank her. They pushed me down to the waiting room in a wheelchair. Sheena was so happy to see me she practically jumped into my lap. I told everyone what had happened and they called Sheena a hero. I never would have made it to the highway without her.

Sheena lived another five years before cancer took her life. It was a very sad time for me. She was a good friend for nine years of my life. I have framed pictures of her, and every time I look at them, I think of the day she helped me.

It has been three years since Sheena died. I have a new friend now, Tucker. He is a two-month-old golden retriever that I hope will always be there for me. I'm going to take him everywhere, just in case.

Heroes

Mary Ellen Bradshaw

In the southern Gulf Islands there is a community spirit, where neighbours help neighbours and friendship is a necessary part of life. It is a place where acts of heroism are commonplace, in part due to the unpredictable sea, the isolation and the weather. The dictionary defines an act of heroism as a courageous and noble act. This tale is about one of these islands and its heroes: a young boy named Matt and his friend, a very large horse named Tonka.

In the early seventies, Tonka and another horse were brought to the island by a couple of young men who planned to build homes and live off the land. The idea was that the horses would earn their keep by pulling logs off the beach. The other horse took to this idea but Tonka, after the first four hours of work, fell down on his side panting and groaning, as if he were having a heart attack. His collapse was a surprise as he was only twelve years old. The next day he seemed in good health, but about two hours into the job, he again fell down, panting. On the third day he fell just as the logging chains were being cinched into place at the start of the work day. It was obvious that heavy labour was not his forte. So from that day on Tonka was free to roam the island.

Some years later the young men gave up their homesteading dream and left the island, taking the workhorse with them. Tonka was left on the island to survive by his own devices. He lived on wild plants, berries and fruit from the old orchards that had been planted by settlers in the late 1800s. He also munched on the flower and vegetable gardens of the residents, paying for his repast with rich, steamy mounds of manure.

Matt, along with his dad, Jim, and his mother, Heather, has lived on this small Gulf Island since birth. He is growing up a child of nature and is being schooled at home by his parents. Matt loves to drop in and chat with the other inhabitants of the tiny community and in doing so has made many friends, most of whom are adults. Of the full-time residents on the island, he is the only child. In many ways he is like a small adult, with some wise insights and a wonderful sense of humour.

Matt had always known and admired Tonka and considered him his own family pet. The horse was a friend, someone to roam the woods with during the long, lonely winters. Matt also has a special human friend, Uncle Barrie, a weekend and summer resident with whom he works side by side, doing chores and learning many useful skills. His favourite thing is running Uncle Barrie's backhoe.

One day, in 1989, while Tonka was making his rounds, he stretched for an apple and stepped onto the wooden cap of one of the original old wells. Unfortunately, the wood was rotten, and Tonka fell through. He was found sometime later by the current owners of the property, who were at a loss about what to do. They gathered some of their island friends and tried to figure a way to get Tonka out.

They decided to call a well-known local healer and her mate from another island. The couple boated over and examined the horse as well as they could under the circumstances. Tonka appeared to be relatively healthy but seemed quite upset about his predicament. They stroked and talked to him and fed him oats and molasses to calm him down. A makeshift sling was made out of an old hammock as they tried to figure out how they were going to get him out of the well.

Someone suggested Barrie's backhoe. Dave and Diane, who share the property with Barrie and his wife, Marlene, happened to be on the island that weekend. Dave found the keys to the backhoe and tried to start it. It would not start. He called Barrie's son, who gave instructions over the phone, but still they could not get it going. Then Dave remembered Matt, the kid who loved nothing better than to drive this stubborn piece of machinery. Matt was summoned, and with his tutelage and a dose of ether, the machine started right away.

They drove the backhoe to the old well. The horse was pulled out, and after examination was found to be thoroughly chilled, but only had a small abrasion on one leg. He was treated with a little antibiotic ointment, a shot of brandy and some blankets. Tonka's life was saved by these resourceful people and a six-year-old hero.

Matt, now age eleven, still lives on the island, but Tonka has become a legend, a part of the island lore. He died at the ripe old age of thirty-two. One day while again pilfering apples, he fell into a mud hole. He was pulled out of the mud with a tractor, only to fall in again. He was pulled out a second time but then fell to the ground and refused to get up. He was covered with blankets and given a shot of brandy. Matt and his father kept an eye on the horse, trying to encourage him to get up.

After a few days, when Tonka had not gotten onto his feet, it was obvious he never would. Sadly, he had to be put out of his misery. Tonka was a very big horse, almost impossible to move, so a wake was held and he was cremated on the spot. The remaining brandy was passed around and suitable toasts were made. Everyone on the island was saddened by their loss, especially Matt. A wooden sign, carved by Barrie and Matt, now marks Tonka's resting place. His spirit continues to roam his beloved island.

Prince and the Hare

Gwendoline S. Mowatt

It was a cold November evening. Snow was falling. My husband and I were quietly reading. Prince lay stretched out in front of the fire. The clock struck nine. Prince let out a "woof" and headed for the door. We waited, expecting a ring, and when none came my husband went to see what it was all about. The moment he opened the door Prince bolted. No amount of calling could bring him back.

Glancing down at the snow we saw large prints. A hare! Oh no! We waited for over an hour, looking out and calling to no avail. We imagined all kinds of things. Poor hare; surely he is being ripped apart. We felt helpless.

Finally a whimper at the door. Opening it we feared the worst, expecting fur and blood dripping from velvet lips — but no, not a trace. Prince wagged his tail, headed for the fireplace and settled down, quite pleased with himself.

For three years it was a nightly ritual: at 9:00 P.M. Prince headed for the door and we let him out. For three years we placed carrots, lettuce and tidbits out, which Hare thankfully received, and for three years Prince and the hare had their nightly romp.

Then the day came when we had to say good-bye to our beagle. He was full of cancer, tormented by pain, no possibility of cure or relief. This we found very difficult to come to terms with — so did Hare.

All that winter we left treats out at 9:00 P.M. sharp. All that winter Hare came to our door but never touched the tidbits. We saw his paw prints in the snow. And then he came no more.

Somehow, somewhere, I feel that when the clock strikes nine a very special hound dog is chasing a very special huge rabbit.

Skunk Radio
Elaine Regier

We always enjoy company, but at the end of summer 1992 we had some very undesirable guests. They arrived one weekend while we were away visiting some friends. We sensed their presence as soon as we entered the house. However, it wasn't until my husband, Bob, slithered into the three-foot crawl space under the house and came nose to nose with two black eyes followed by a long white stripe that we knew a family of skunks had moved in. The pressure on Bob to evict the skunks was intensified by the fact that we had invited our church fellowship over for a corn roast the next weekend.

We began investigating our options. Live traps, we discovered, could be rented for $70 per week per skunk — but what do you do with a trapped skunk without arousing its suspicions or its defence mechanisms? A pest control company would remove them for us at $150 per skunk. A lower-priced alternative was offered by the S.P.C.A. They suggested that since skunks like it dark and quiet, we could try to create a hostile environment with lights and radios, preferably talk shows.

So Bob did just that. He rounded up a contingent of radios and lights and placed them under the house. Then we, too, lived with CKNW blaring at top volume for forty-eight straight hours. At the end of that time, Bob again went under the house. He was pleased to discover that the unwelcome guests had left to find more suitable accommodation.

The Bomb That Mooed

Howard White

When I was five my family, consisting of my parents, my two sisters and myself, moved to Green Bay, a tiny logging camp on one of British Columbia's more out-of-the-way Gulf Islands. Unlike settlers on the more popular islands, up at Green Bay we felt virtually without neighbours. Technically speaking we had some, the Henrys. The Henrys were an old-world Finnish couple, and I think the term my father used for them was "hard-bitten." They had the old cannery site in the little hole-in-the-wall just to the right as you came out of the main bay. There were still a number of cannery cabins scattered along the beach bluffs, which the Henrys organized into a sort of low-budget summer resort, mainly for Finn mill workers from Fraser Mills in New Westminster.

As Finns tend to be, the Henrys were inexhaustibly hard-working, especially Mrs. Henry. Boats leaving camp at daybreak would always discover her out before them, jigging for cod off the bay mouth in one of the curiously designed sampan-like boats they used. During the spring she toiled until dusk in the large garden they had built up on a rock knoll near their house, laboriously packing soil in pails and fertilizing it with starfish, dogfish and seaweed until it blossomed into a heartbreaking jungle of fruits, berries and vegetables — heartbreaking because, gawk and drool as we might, we can-fed urchins never got to sample a bit of it. Every scrap of food Mrs. Henry could lay her hands on went into jars to feed her summer guests.

The locals warned Dad that the two old Finns were "mesatchie" — an old Chinook word for ornery — so, true to his perverse nature, he set out to win them over. This proved less than simple. Some of those old first-generation Finns had a very hard face which they turned to the non-Finnish world, a peculiar expression so blanched of feeling as to be completely intimidating, and this was the face we would be met with on any attempt to stop the Henrys for a chat on the Irvine's Landing dock, or to drop in on them for a casual visit. One's business would be crisply asked, and there being none of note, no quarter would be given. The seven-mile trip to the nearest town, Pender Harbour, was a day's undertaking in those slow-moving days, particularly with the Henrys' snail-like little sampans, but all overtures towards collaborating on shopping runs were dismissed without consideration. The initial attempt to deliver their accumulated winter mail was received with something akin to shock, and resulted in the postmaster being rudely dressed down and ordered not to allow it again.

There was one crack in the Henrys' heavily armoured independence, however: their cow.

The trouble with the Henrys' cow was it was Canadian. They wanted a Finnish cow as frugal and orderly as they were, but this cow was haywire. For one thing it gave too much milk, and always at the wrong time, so Mrs. Henry had lots when there were no guests to feed and none when there were lots. This led to an actual attempt to acknowledge our neighbourly existence, which took the form of her approaching my mother with an offer to provide the camp with fresh milk. Mom of course happily agreed, even when she found out the old lady wanted the same price per ounce as canned milk at Murdoch's store. Mom took it and even kept taking it after we discovered it was so queer-tasting, a result of her cow's peculiar diet of seaweed and salal brush, that no one would drink it, so anxious was she to establish something approaching a normal human relationship with her only neighbour.

The other thing about Mrs. Henry's cow that helped bring us together was its propensity for wandering. There was no real road connecting our two places — they wouldn't let Dad make one — and Mrs. Henry desperately tried to keep it fenced and roped in, but that cow was over at our place every time you turned around. I don't know why. It just hung around. I think maybe it longed to hear its own language spoken. We kids naturally liked it and made a big fuss over it and snuck it pocketfuls of rolled oats, but Mom and Dad made a neighbourly effort to send it home. Dad was afraid a logging truck would run over it and he'd have to pay Mrs. Henry its worth in T-bone steaks at Murdoch's store. The trouble was, it was very hard for the cow to get home. It would get bogged down in swamps, jam its head between close-spaced saplings and get stuck trying to climb over fallen logs, bawling and thrashing as spike knots dug into its udder. We could never figure out how it got around on its own or why it was never killed by a cougar or one of the areas's numerous pit-lampers.

The cow's greatest caper was the time it ate the dynamite. Dad was a bit sensitive about the dynamite, because by law it was supposed to be kept locked up in a special airtight magazine built out of six-inch by six-inch timbers, while he had it stashed in a flimsy open lean-to just up the road from the shop. On top of this, you were supposed to destroy dynamite after a certain date because it becomes unstable and dangerous to handle, but he could never bring himself to just burn dynamite he'd paid good money for. Eventually ours got so old and cranky everybody was afraid to go within a hundred feet of the magazine, let alone use the stuff. This was when Mrs. Henry's cow was discovered standing by the road chewing away on a stick of 20-per-cent stumping powder as contentedly as Fidel Castro munching a Havana cigar. Closer inspection revealed that the beast had been living for some days at the magazine, stomping boxes open and eating case after case of dynamite, evidently enjoying the piquant taste of saltpetre-and-nitroglycerine-soaked sawdust.

"Holy jumped-up, bald-headed, bare-assed, black-balled Mexican Christ!" my father shouted, twisting his cap around on his head as the implications of the discovery sunk in. "Nobody touch that cow!"

"One hiccup and we're goners," observed Jack Spence, the sardonic foreman. "Can you imagine what a time the cops would have trying to figure it out? Just a crater full of guts, hoofs and hardhats."

They were afraid the cow would go home and blow up in Mrs. Henry's barn, or else the dynamite would get into the milk and poison half the crew of Fraser Mills. Finally they decided to drive it way to hell and gone up the logging road where it would take two weeks to get home, by which time it should have cleaned its system out. But nobody wanted to go close enough to tie a rope around its neck, so they hit on the idea of getting behind it with the logging truck and scaring it up the road with the air horn. With everyone else cowering down behind stumps, Tom Grey eased slowly up in the truck, but at the first blast the unsuspecting animal shot into the brush like a goosed kangaroo and was gone. We all spent the following week with one ear tuned for large blasts, actual or verbal, emanating from the Henrys' direction, but the case of the bomb that mooed closed without further incident.

Pig
Leona Gom

They say you make a good pet
    (I have seen you taken for walks
    on a leash in a Major American City
    with a red bow around your neck)
They say you are more intelligent than dogs
    (Yes — dogs have the I.Q. of Q-tips)
They say you are a good watchpig
    (I imagine you crouching wary
    at night in my living room
    baring your teeth)
They say beauty is in a pig's eye

There is no doubt
your image has changed

Someday I will sit in my senile city chair
and tell stories to your descendants
sitting on their bored haunches at my feet
    of the barbaric days
when you were bred for food
like the first Pekinese
    of unjust epithets
like "wallowing" and "filthy"
ascribed to you
    of you anarchic through fences
plundering gardens
and galloping gracelessly down country roads
with us in furious pursuit
    of all those unenlightened days
when we were simply farmers
and you were simply swine

III: In From the Wild

Whale Watching

Sandy Shreve

for Andrea Lebowitz

All week we search through sightings
of seals and otters
and lost logs in the water
for the orcas

Hoping to see fins in the distance
binoculars raised
we whisk our eyes across wave
after wave, wish away the constant
ferries and outboards
want the channel a calm
invitation for whales

as if our seeing them
would be proof of possibility
that all we have inflicted
on this world
might be reversed
and all the ruin changed
to an unscathed grace

as if the common seal
no longer counts enough for this
approaches going home
with a story of sea gulls
instead of eagles

Do we want the rare, endangered
species to visit us
to bestow some special privilege
like a trust
that tells us we are not
the culprits

I want to believe it's something else
this longing for the exotic
something that transcends
such tired desires

Of course, the time comes
when we give up
accept a pattern of metallic slaps
as one more shipping sound
Engrossed in books we let it pass
until by accident of a glance
we glimpse the last three whales
breaching in the bay just yards away

We gaze, trapped between elation and regret
in that moment luck has granted —
kicking ourselves for what we missed
we still feel honoured by the orcas
who likely neither know nor care
that we are, wistful, there
wishing they'd come back
give us one more chance

The Great Bear Trial
William Deverell

Our car sweeps around a bend, and we see an entire mountain stripped. From Nanaimo through Port Alberni, across the crooked spine of Vancouver Island to the wild western shores, you see many such clearcuts, ragged sores upon the face of our 100-per-cent non-recyclable planet.

"Beautiful B.C.," says Jeff Green. He is a trial lawyer from Victoria, one of several friends from my own lawyering days who are meeting in Tofino to defend some bear huggers charged with disrupting a trophy hunt. Jeff won't be charging a fee. He says he is doing it for the bear minimum.

I am coming as The Press, and the story I have been sold on is this: (1) Eight eco-activists disrupted a legal hunt last April. (2) The head and hide of a giant black bear were stolen from the hunters. (3) A native man hid these furry remains in a sacred cave after a ceremony to free the bear's spirit.

The eight persons charged are members of the Friends of Clayoquot Sound, a largely ad hoc group of local environmentalists who believe in putting themselves on the line. In the case I am to witness, they proudly bear (so to speak) the blame. And may bear the brunt.

Between 4,000 and 5,000 black bears a year are legally killed in British Columbia. It is not known how many are illegally killed, but poaching is a growing concern — in Asia, bear-paw pads make a tasty soup, claws are decorator items, and the genitalia are thought to induce sexual arousal. The gall bladders, used for intestinal and liver ailments, are an especially hot item on the other side of the Pacific Rim, worth as much as $5,000 each in Korea. The Asian bear population has been nearly destroyed because of this. That is what the World Wildlife Fund says, according to a clipping I have from the *Globe and Mail*.

In my file there is also a press release written by Julie Draper, one of the accused, a vocal member of the Friends of Clayoquot Sound. "Bear populations are plummeting in North America," she says. "The loss of habitat through development and deforestation is enormous." She has quoted part of a speech ascribed to the great Salish chief, Seattle: "If I decide to accept your offer to buy our land, I will make one condition. The white man must treat the beasts of this land as his brothers. I am a savage and do not understand any other way. If beasts were gone, men would die from great loneliness of spirit, for whatever happens to the beasts also happens to the man. All things are connected. Whatever befalls the earth, befalls the sons of the earth."

Another naked hillside looms ahead...

All things are connected. I am curious to learn about that sacred Indian cave, the ritual to raise the spirit of the bear.

We pull into Tofino, capital of the so-called Hippie Coast and a town of cedar-shingled charm. It nests in a bay of islands near Pacific Rim National Park, and on a sunny day you can see Meares Island to the north, and beyond it, white ridges and snow-cones. Behind the beauty, beneath the calm, there is tension: people here are preparing for what they call the last stand — anti-logging blockades in nearby Clayoquot Sound.

At the docks of the Weigh West Resort, Jeff and I shout and wave to Rod Palm, who lives on Strawberry Island. Mr. Palm, one of the accused, runs a tour boat and whale-watching business. After he motors across to pick us up in his big aluminum skiff, I get a good look at this eco-terrorist. He is fifty-one, balding, soft-spoken, shy.

Last April, he was racing his skiff down a channel, hooting his horn to scare the bears from the shore. (April is when black bears are easiest to find. They wobble from their dens hungry, weak and almost blind, and they head to the water to feed on shore life. The hunters, as Jeff explained to me, arrive in boats. "They stand beside the boat and shoot a bear until it is dead so that later they can look at its head on the wall of their den. This is intended to give them a form of manly pleasure.")

A tricky manoeuvre between submerged rocks brings us to the shore of Wickaninnish Island, and the summer home of my ex-partner, David Gibbons. The spacious house is dwarfed by the twisted trees that hover over it like giant gargoyles, thick-waisted cedars and hemlocks that have suffered uneven battle with the Pacific storms.

David comes out to help us unload our bags. I have known him for almost thirty years and remember when he was thinner. He isn't the kind of guy who flashes his ego in court, but he has a gentle Irish wit and is as smooth as satin.

David, too, is donating his services to the bear people, as he calls them. He promises me he will cross-examine the hunters about the traffic in bear parts. He assures me he is going to ask: "So this bear died in order to help some Korean gentleman get a hard-on?"

Peter Ritchie is already here. I have also known him a long time — from the days when he was still a prosecutor, before he went straight. Peter has come here from a drug-smuggling case in San Francisco to defend the bear people. Like the others, he is paying his own expenses.

John Green finally arrives, Jeff's brother and law partner. We gather around David's massive cedar table, sleeves rolled up, and the lawyers get to work. The main witnesses, I learn, are a licenced outfitter from Port Alberni, his assistant guide, and two hunters from California. Their evidence: protesters raced up and down a channel in two boats blaring their horns to scare off bears, and later others blocked the hunters' access to a boat ramp, while two men stole the head and hide of a freshly killed bear, and spirited these away in one of the boats. Multiple counts of theft, mischief, dangerous boating and interfering with a lawful hunt.

The witnesses will also say Steve Lawson admitted concealing the bear hide in the secret cave after a ceremony in which he asked it to forgive its killers. Mr. Lawson is a treaty Indian. He already has three convictions for interfering in bear hunts. (In 1988 the hide of a nursing mother was found at a local dump and some motherless cubs were seen near the national park, starving and eating grass. Thirteen other bears were killed during that hunt. Mr. Lawson tried to stop it and a judge fined him and his compatriots $1,500 each.)

The case seems difficult. The clients are proud eco-recidivists, veterans of many logging blockades for which some even served time for contempt of court. And during their police interviews they'd eagerly confessed. But in the defence business, the most important aspect of a case often has nothing to do with the facts — or with the law, for that matter. It has to do with capturing the heart and mind of the judge. In this case, perhaps the only hope is that the judge is a closet environmentalist.

"Hey, guys," says David, "in court I'm going to refer to this as the skin trade."

"Killing for entertainment is the way I want to put it," says Jeff.

The evening descends into frivolity. There is wordplay. The Crown is going to be em*bear*assed. New business cards will be printed: "Bearisters and solicitors." John says he can't bear any more wine. Jeff opens a twelve-pack and suggests we kill a few bears. Later, loaded (for bear), we go outside and look at the stars. Peter identifies the constellation above us. It is Ursa Major, the Great Bear.

I feel the spirit of the bear watching us, and become uneasy. *Whatever happens to the beasts also happens to the man.*

Daffodils and tulips and magnolias bloom in the front yards of Tofino on this sunny mid-April Monday. The townsfolk stare solemnly at the four black suits walking down the main drag, protectors of the bear people, here to take on the local law. At the municipal hall, which doubles as Tofino's courthouse, we are joined by Ted Holekamp, from Courtenay, Steve Lawson's friend and lawyer.

A dozen smiling children are standing in front of the municipal hall. Little Sirena Flemming carries a sign that says, "My daddy protects bears." Other kids wave similar placards: "Quit killing wildlife for fun." "Pacific Plunderland." A CTV camera records this.

In the council chambers, it's standing room only, forty-five men, women and children, some in native Indian dress. The windows here face north, and you can see the green tresses of the hills, gulls flipping through the air. You can hear dogs barking and children playing.

The judge enters to a great shuffling of feet and scraping of chairs. Judge Klaver looks like an outdoorsman, handsome, rangy, a salt and pepper beard.

The first witness is Darren De Luca, the assistant guide. You can tell that Mr. De Luca is proud of what he does. "I took thirty bears last year," he says. The hide that was stolen, he tells us, was from "easily a record-book bear, a B.C. record." His hunter client shot the bear from fifty yards away. "I kicked it a couple of times, put the barrel in its eyes, and it was dead."

David asks him: "You sort of like to get them just after hibernation, when they're coming down to the water?"

"That's one way." If the bear is eating at the shore, he explains, you set "an ambush."

After skinning this bear he left its remains on the beach, which he says is the usual practice. "Mostly just eagles will take the remains," he says, "usually gone within three days."

And the gall bladders?

"I'm instructed to recover them. Wayne would freeze the gall bladders and sell them for the Asians."

Outside on the grass, during the break, I tell Darren De Luca I bet he's glad that's over. "They didn't do nothing to me," he says. "Them lawyers ain't so hot." A pleasant middle-aged woman from Courtenay presents all the accused with engraved soup spoons. "Bear Defender 1993," they read.

Back in court, the trial takes a sudden turn. The Crown is unable to prove Steve Lawson's statements about his role as receiver of the stolen bear hide, and proceedings are stayed against him. The court erupts in applause. The judge isn't amused. He says, "I didn't realize we were playing some sort of game here, with people cheering for one side or another."

"It's more than a game," says someone in the gallery.

The judge glares.

I have lunch with Steve Lawson at the Alley Way Cafe. He is forty-four, builds boats and runs charters and has six children. He is Ojibwa, from Kenora, Ontario, but tells me he has been in B.C. since he was four, and grew up in foster homes and institutions before being adopted by his psychologist. His wife, Susanne Hare, is also a prominent activist. After a logging protest in 1989 they took turns serving eight days in Oakalla so one of them could be with the children. He is articulate and widely read, gentle, centred.

"Throughout all native cultures of North America the bear spirit is perceived as the protector and healer," he says. "So the hide was brought to me and taken into my home, and he was fêted — food was offered, and his presence was honoured around us. Living, that bear would have been magnificent, and at the beginning, the energy surrounding him was filled with shock and rage. We tried to explain to the bear that his life was not given up for frivolous reasons. On behalf of the hunter, because he, like us, was human, we apologized. After that, even my children noticed the bear's energy change. His features softened. His energy was satisfied and his spirit was appeased. It was a form of completion."

At dawn the next morning, the head and hide were taken by boat to a cave he had discovered near Tofino when helping an archaeologist. It was a place of ceremony, he believes, a sacred place. "Native people from here had placed skulls of bears at the back of the cave. I couldn't tell the police where it was because I was bound by the people who used it and by the elders' beliefs."

He is convinced the spirit of this bear rewarded him with his innocence. "I've lost on every other occasion on the environmental front. This might be a turnaround. In a spiritual sense the bear returned something to me. His spirit was speaking through the lawyers."

In court, we hear from one of the hunters, a broad-shouldered jeweller from San Diego who says his boat was almost swamped by the protesters' larger vessel. He tells how the outfitter's boat trailer was obstructed by Julie Draper at the public ramp as she stood there vigorously making her views known. For this she has been charged with mischief. He testifies one of the protesters grabbed his trophy kill and raced off in a boat with it. The hunters were forced to abandon their sport after that, but Wayne Weibe, the outfitter, later killed another bear for him, and sent the head and hide to him in San Diego.

His and others' accounts of the outfitter's oathings and expletives later at the RCMP station hint that Mr. Weibe is a man of brisk temper. He was bellowing, pointing out the protesters, insisting they be charged and thrown in jail. During an adjournment I see him standing outside with a few of his guides, smoking, scowling. He is forty-eight, and he looks sort of like a bear himself, thick of girth, sloping shoulders, grey curls.

Willie Sport, an elder of the Ohiaht people of this coast who has been in court all day with his wife, tells me they are here to give moral support. Mr. Sport is sixty-nine, and knowledge has been passed on to him by his grandfather, a shaman.

"In my village we do not have totems. We have a bear figure and a human figure at the corners of our lodges. We believe the bear is the closest animal to human, the most sacred animal, more sacred than anything else that lives, next to man. We believe we get our strength and power from the bear. The only time my people will kill a bear is when they are really hungry, and then we'll watch it for a week and make sure it doesn't have cubs. We have a ceremony before we kill it. We never shoot for pleasure."

He adds: "When it's dying it sounds like a human being in pain."

He speaks of reincarnation. "We believe the bear will return as an eagle, a raven, a wolf. We all have spirits, even that blade of grass."

That evening, after a walk through the forest and a sauna, Peter Ritchie tells me that while Willie Sport was talking to me he overheard Mr. Weibe say, "He's feeding him all that Indian shit."

As we squeeze into the courtroom the next day, John Green says, "Open season on bear hunters this morning."

Mr Weibe, who is surprisingly muted on the stand, says he has a licence from the government to outfit hunts through most of northern Vancouver Island and employs seven assistant guides.

"Last year we run a hundred per cent on our bear hunt. Eighty-three bears last year." He charges each hunter $2,850 U.S. for the first bear, $1,000 for a second, and pretty well guarantees a kill. He feels the provincial government does well by him: he earned them $20,000 in royalties last year.

After Mr. Weibe tells his story of the honking horns and the blockade at the ramp, he's turned over to the defence, and now David Gibbons gets his chance to ask about bear parts.

Yes, Mr. Weibe used to take the gall bladders, but he is vague about what he did with them. "I keep them and sell them or give them away. It's now unlawful."

How much do you get for them? "I heard $3,000, but mine only went for $200."

Who did he sell them to? "A guy in Las Vegas, a Mr. No. He used to send me customers from Korea."

Who is this inscrutable Mr. No? Does Agent 007 know about this? But David doesn't follow it up, and simply asks, "I hear men use those for sexual purposes."

Mr. Weibe allows as he's heard something to that effect, and he grins. But Judge Klaver, the former schoolteacher, is frowning, and David backs off.

Jeff asks him if he's aware there is a growing opposition to killing bears for entertainment purposes. Mr. Weibe says he wouldn't call it entertainment purposes. "I sell a hunt."

"Is it considered fun? Fun to kill those bears?"

"You can have fun a lot cheaper," says Mr. Weibe.

Jeff asks him to comment on an article in the *Globe* about black bears being endangered. "I don't read a whole bunch," he answers. "I don't pore over the papers about black bears."

Outside, he is in better form. "I'm sick and tired of these guys protesting my hunt. Those lawyers in there are trying to dick around with my evidence, bunch of guys in a suit trying to make a bozo out of me." He is colourful when not restrained by the niceties of the court-room. He is a character. And you have to see his point of view — hunting is his life, his livelihood, this is what he has known.

"I happen to admire black bears," he tells me. "They're a neat animal to watch, my favourite animal." He explains he's a conservationist; he fought for the new anti-bear parts law to discourage poaching. He says the annual bear hunt in B.C. is worth $600,000 to the government, not including hotels, restaurants and airlines.

I ask if he intends to hunt in this area after the trial. "Business as usual around here," he says.

In his summation, David makes a pitch for the rights of protest. "In our country we have to tolerate conversations about philosophy. We ought to encourage our citizenry to have vigorous debates on important issues. People shouldn't be branded as criminals because they stood on a boat ramp for five minutes and had a conversation about the skin trade."

At the end of all this the judge reserves decision and makes an enigmatic comment: "Well, I guess I'm the perfect person to hear this because I used to be a hunter but I haven't for many years."

The lawyers gather in the parking lot. What was the judge implying? Is he a hunter still at heart? Have his views changed? No one is sure. The key to the trial still involves winning the heart of this judge, but he remains a mystery.

The final day of the Great Bear Trial is scheduled for late August and will be heard not in Tofino but in Port Alberni.

Judge Klaver, for reasons given a few months earlier, has already dismissed a few of the charges but convicted six of the protestors. Robert Flemming, a thirty-two-year-old welder and machinist, faces a possible jail term: he was found guilty of theft of the bear hide. In his plea for leniency, John Green reminds the judge the theft was not for profit but because his client took issue with someone's determination to "blast away at defenceless animals."

The prosecutor asks that in sentencing Flemming he be ordered to reimburse the hunter for the value of the hide. It should be assessed "not only in economic but in sentimental terms to the hunter."

John suggests the bear was also sentimentally attached to the hide.

Judge Klaver doesn't smile. To this point we still can't read whether he is a hammer or a man of gentler passion.

The lawyers expect the worst, but after all the speeches are in, Klaver, with barely a word of admonition to anyone, gives Flemming an unexpected reward, a discharge: no criminal record. A dangerous boater gets rapped for $500 but everyone else is fined only a token hundred. The accused relax. The lawyers relax.

Now Klaver has something he wants to get off his chest. He says, "This case has given me a great number of sleepless nights." He hints he held some personal views but had to "leave my personal feelings out of it." He reminds us of his comment that he is no longer a hunter. There is a sense he wants to say more but feels constrained. He is a judge; he must do his duty.

Outside court, there are bear hugs all around. There is talk of strategies for when the bear hunters return.

On the drive home, I read more oratory of Chief Seattle: his reply in 1854 to the Great White Chief in Washington, who had promised a "reservation" for his people.

"We know that the white man does not understand our ways. One portion of land is the same to him as the next, for he is a stranger who comes in the night and takes from the land whatever he needs. He treats his mother, the earth, and his brother, the sky, as things to be bought, plundered, sold like sheep or bright beads. His appetite will devour the earth and leave behind only a desert."

How sad is this reproachful poetry, I think, how prophetic his melancholic words.

"This we know: The earth does not belong to man; man belongs to the earth. All things are connected like the blood which unites one family. All things are connected."

Day of the Cephalopod
Catherine Lebredt

It was one of those mornings in late May when the retreating waters of a minus tide leave acres of yellow-green mudflats exposed and steaming under a warm spring sun.

From our float-house vantage point, in a tiny, ebb-tide pond encircled by mudflats rising steeply on three sides, we sat, sipping our morning coffee, enjoying the antics of our four-footed neighbours: a pair of ringtailed raccoons diligently pulling long pink worms from the seldom accessible reaches of the low-tide line; a playful otter, belly-riding down her slick mud slide and disappearing with a whoosh into the depths of a cool green sea. Occasionally, a bald eagle swooped down to pluck bite-sized perch from the tidal pool, an offering for the hungry eaglet waiting impatiently in a treetop nest.

For years we have watched the comings and goings of these creatures with whom we share Maltby Slough. And every once in a while, something odd or unexpected occurs, reminding us how unpredictable and unexplainable nature can be, and above all, how little we know of her strange ways. This was one of those mornings.

As I rose to begin my chores, something on an adjacent mudflat caught my eye. A long, irregular pink shape was slowly making its way across the muddy expanse. Grabbing binoculars for a closer look, I zeroed in on this astonishing sight. An octopus! It couldn't be, could it?

Jumping into the canoe, my husband, Mike, paddled over to the edge of the mudflat, then slogged across the oozing muck until he reached the stranded creature. It was indeed an octopus — about a thirty-pounder, five to six feet in length. With some difficulty the slippery cephalopod was gently deposited into the only available container — a five-gallon bucket — and transported back to the float house. Quickly we pulled the canoe up on a deck and began filling it with sea water. When this makeshift holding tank was ready, we poured the weakened octopus out of the bucket and into the water-filled canoe.

The creature was so weak, it appeared to be near death. Its colour was pale and washed out, not the bright red that would normally be exhibited in a frightened or angry octopus. Nonetheless, ripples of pink washed over the strange body and horny bumps rose up on its skin. We were filled with compassion for this eight-legged alien. Its fear was evident, but how were we to console a being so unlike ourselves?

Jacques Cousteau once referred to the octopus as "the soft intelligence," for, exclusive of marine mammals, the octopus is the most intelligent creature in the sea. Although feared and persecuted by humans for centuries, it is a shy, often gentle creature with a great capacity to learn, reason and remember. And it has often shown a willingness to befriend human beings.

With these thoughts in mind, I reached out and stroked its cool, elastic skin. Ripples of colour passed over its body at my touch. It was then that I noticed our friend was one leg short. Had this recent injury contributed to its weakened state? Our seven-year-old daughter leaned close and offered reassuring words. Perhaps it knew we meant it no harm. Covering the canoe with boards to create a cave-like retreat, we left it alone for the remainder of the day.

By the evening, the octopus had recovered enough energy to pry the bulkhead out of the bow of the canoe in an attempt to retreat even further into the dark. We decided it was time to release our charge.

While Mike took hold of the body, I took the legs — not an easy task for the inexperienced. We struggled over to the edge of the deck and lowered the cephalopod into the sea. With a mixture of fascination and regret we watched it spread its graceful flowing form like a parachute, then slowly descend into the darkness of its own familiar world.

Phil, the Fearless Pheasant
Gloria Danyluk

Anyone who is familiar with ring-necked pheasants knows that they are always running away from everyone and everything. Well, I know of one male pheasant who not only didn't shy away but gave chase.

About four years ago, when I was working as a flight instructor, this particular pheasant started chasing aircraft. He showed no fear at all, running alongside sometimes right by the wheels. This bird was so bold, chasing aircraft many times his size, that we named him Phil, the fearless pheasant. I knew that male pheasants are very protective of their territory, but why he would consider a portion of asphalt his property is a mystery. At the airport where I worked, his nest was along a creek that was about a hundred feet from the side of the runway. It was quite comical to see his head pop up above the grass when he heard an airplane taxiing down the runway and then started charging towards you dodging bumps and hollows. Sometimes in his haste to chase he would fly over, then hit the ground running.

Because aircraft are always leaving a runway, taxiing in or taking off, one can see why he kept doing this. We were constantly reinforcing his behaviour. He really did think he was getting rid of these "pests."

I have a theory about Phil's urge to chase. About a year before he was noticed, a student and I were taking off when I noticed some brown blobs on the runway. As we were getting closer, I realized the blobs were baby pheasants. We managed to miss them, and when I looked back Mama Pheasant was shooing her brood back to the grass. She probably thought we were a very large hawk. I figured Phil must have been one of those babies, and now he was seeking revenge for being frightened.

Occasionally he would get a little too close and accidentally get bumped by a wheel, but he would always come back. It seemed to harden his resolve to keep chasing. Other times he would actually wait on the runway as you prepared for take-off. Then, as you streaked by him, sometimes missing him by inches, he'd start running after you. It always seemed to me as if he was daring you to run over him.

One winter he injured his leg, probably by tripping over his own feet. He kept it tucked under his belly, standing only on one leg. Even this injury didn't stop him from chasing. As if to say, "I may be down but I'm not out," he made an effort to run on one leg, using his wing like a crutch. One has to give the bird credit for being so persistent.

Unfortunately, once his leg got better, he met his demise. An aircraft ran over him. No injuries to the plane, but Phil was no more. I was sorry to see him go and glad it wasn't me who had hit him. I always considered him a buddy, a friend out to greet me as I went down the runway. Now I miss him. He even had the distinction of being the airport mascot.

Now that he has passed on to the next life, maybe he will be what I sometimes thought he wanted to be — an airplane!

The Kiss
Michael David Johnson

One day I came home from school. I was on the couch watching TV when my brother, Paul, ran around to the back door and said, "Michael, Michael, there is a mouse at the front door!" We quickly ran to the front door. I said, "Paul, that is not a mouse, that's a rat!" My brother and I ran to the back yard where my dad was mowing the lawn. I said, "Dad, there's a rat at the front door!" My dad went to the front yard to see the rat. When he saw the rat, he took a broom and swept it away, thinking it was a wild rat. The rat ran off. But later on it came back.

After a while, we began to think it was someone's pet which got loose. We began thinking how my cat, Gracie, would react when seeing it. Then my dad told me to go get my cat. I asked, "Why do you want me to?" My dad said, "I want to see what she'll do." I said, "Dad, that's mean. She'll kill the rat." Then he said, "No, I don't think she will." So I went in the house and got my cat. I came back outside and handed Gracie to my dad. We then put her on the fence where the rat was. My cat sat on the fence. Then the two made eye contact.

Then, all of a sudden, my cat slowly bent over and kissed the rat on the nose! My dad, my brother and I burst out into laughter. That is why, to this very day, every time I think about that time or tell about it, I still laugh!

Our Bear Cat
Holly Barber Pugsley

I grew up a dog lover, never having known the wonderful friendship a cat can give. One day, though, I made eye contact with the cutest kitten I had ever seen. I had to have her, and my husband said sure. She then became a part of our family for seventeen years.

Belle was the size of an eight-week-old kitten even though she was five or six months old. She was an underfed ranch kitten who would never have survived the winter. She had spirit and an irresistible look to her, and we took her home and thoroughly enjoyed her.

Always a very small cat, Belle never weighed more than four pounds. Her most daring adventure came when she was fifteen years old and weighed a mere three and a half pounds.

It was a cool day in August in Williams Lake, but the sun was still warm. I went outside to soak up some warmth. Sitting on a rock about fifty feet from the house, I started to read my book. As usual, Belle was always near, and when she saw me she came over to pester me for a pet. She purred and pushed her head at me as I read on.

It was beautifully quiet, calm the rule of the moment. Then, as I reached over to stroke Belle again, she growled so deep and low that she shocked me. I looked up at her, but she wasn't looking at me. I followed her gaze over to the corner of the house, and not more than sixty feet away was a black bear.

As I started to stand, Belle took off towards the bear, slinking low and moving rapidly like a hunting cat. The bear stood up on his hind legs, looking over the situation. I started waving my arms and yelling at the bear to leave. Next is the picture I will forever carefully guard in my mind: there is my dear Belle, bravely poised at the feet of the bear, on her tiptoes, back sharply arched, tail crooked and fur sticking straight out, taking her stand to scare him away.

With all the commotion I was causing, the bear probably hadn't even noticed this tiny beauty approaching him. He had evidently seen enough and started coming down to earth with his big front paws. Those paws came within inches of Belle as she stoutly stood her ground. It was then that the bear spotted her. In a flash, he swung off to his left and climbed the nearest tree.

I could hardly believe what I had seen, but I took the opportunity to run into the house and get Den, my husband, yelling "Belle treed a bear! Belle treed a bear!"

Going back outside, we saw the bear just hit the ground. Den clapped his hands and yelled at the old bruin, and the animal slowly ambled away.

We wondered what in the world had happened to Belle. We started calling her and looking for her in her usual hiding place, the woodpile. Sure enough, she had taken her opportunity to run away too. She came out of the safety of the woodpile when she heard us call.

There she was, our adorable, loving, loyal cat. Her semi-long hair stuck out straight from her body in all directions. She walked at our feet looking like that for a full fifteen minutes.

Her bravery and loyalty went beyond normal after that, too. Although at times she made me feel rather childlike, after that incident Belle was my very attentive personal guardian. She went with me everywhere outside, ever alert for any threat to me. When I sat to pull weeds, she would always be there to watch my back. Often she would stare at the spot where she had faced the beast over sixty times her size.

To say that we miss her since she died is a gross understatement. Although we have two other cats now, Belle will always be our irreplaceable bear cat.

On Parade
Kit Gifford

For many years our home in an isolated spot on Masset Inlet, in the Queen Charlotte Islands, has been a wildlife sanctuary. We have chosen not to post the land, feeling that this can lead to some degree of antagonism in the local freedom-loving hunter population. Rather, we talk with people, intercepting persons who arrive somewhere on our lengthy stretch of beach, hunting rifle in hand and the pulse of the quest in their hearts. We have come to be able to judge the distance of the sound of a rifle shot to a nicety, and have many times gone loping off through the bush to intercept and educate a potential hunter. It has worked well.

Our daughter and I have also been involved in a fair amount of wildlife salvage work, and work it certainly is. She has healed, raised, fed and otherwise nurtured, then released back to the wild, any number of birds and animals. Our family of domestic pets has grown quite accustomed to undomestic creatures sharing their hearth and home.

At the time in question, we had a young adult Doberman who had been raised with a family of Canada geese and with orphaned fawns, plus other birds of assorted personalities. And one of the family cats was a constant companion of all these critters as well as being a devoted companion on walks in forest or along the beach. At the time, mid-autumn, of this adventure, we were weaning a pair of fawns that followed us everywhere in hope of another bite of food. Life was also enlivened by two adolescent crows that had fallen out of their nests at a far-too-early age. These birds had been hand-fed too, often in company with a gaggle of goslings, and all were totally devoted to either my daughter or me out of intense cupboard love. They flew like angels.

One afternoon we heard the sound of rifle shots not quite far enough down the beach to be certainly out of the sanctuary area, so we got ourselves together to go do our missionary work with the hunter. The dog, who simply adored the sight and/or sound of a gun, was leaping eagerly in anticipation. My daughter and I each carried a .22 rifle simply because this had been decided as one of the rules of such an exercise. We set off and hiked briskly along the beach for a bit, then realized we were not alone. We only headed the parade. Beside and between us loped the Doberman, thrilled to pieces with the whole idea. Directly behind us came two still-spotted young deer, ears pricked eagerly for the fun of a walk on the beach. Behind them trotted a blue-point Siamese cat, tail in the air and whiskers bristling. In the shallow water, just offshore beside us, paddled a flotilla of Canada goslings, then about five months old and still very much attached to their mom, my daughter. And around our heads flew two loud, raucous, insistent black birds, who landed briefly and indiscriminately on heads, shoulders, dog, deer, rifle butts, driftwood and beach boulders. Suddenly my daughter and I looked at each other, after trying in vain to shoo this menagerie back in the direction of home; looked at each other and collapsed in hoots and shouts of hysterical laughter. We laughed until we wept, finally laughed ourselves into weakness, flopped there on the beach logs, all with a concerned and caring audience of dog, deer, cat and birds — and decided to abort the mission. No hunter could take seriously this assortment of creatures, up to and including the two crazy ladies who led the parade. We turned and went home, with the disappointed animals, wild and domestic, trailing along behind.

From the Bathroom Window
Reene Granlin

The sky is low and colourless, and where it meets the grey snow at the top of the ridge, the horizon blurs, then disappears, while the sun sits behind the hill planning an attack on the haze. The willows, which often show some green by this time of year, are still grey and brown, making good camouflage for a young moose picking her way along the face of the hill. Each step is laboured and hesitant as she moves in and out of the half-light, aiming for a red osier clump. From the bathroom window, I track her through binoculars, sensing something is wrong. After several minutes she heaves herself into the open, trying to gain altitude, only to break through the snow's crust. Now she offers me a clear view of her backside and its awkward support — a set of mismatched rear legs, the left several centimetres shorter than the right. I move the glasses over her bony body and focus on her long thin face.

"There's something wrong with our moose!" I call, hearing Marc coming up from the basement. "That's an understatement," I think, as I pass him the field glasses. There has always been something wrong with this moose. The first time we saw her, an uncoordinated, sickly looking calf, standing beside her mother in these same willows, we had no idea that three years later we would still be watching her antics. The bleak morning adds the right touch of drama to another episode of her story, which takes place in the countryside near our home in northwestern British Columbia.

Our viewing spot suddenly feels crowded when Paul and Ingrid join us. "I think she walks funny because the snow's too crunchy." Paul's five-year-old optimism comes through as he scans the hillside through the glasses. Ingrid catches my eye and raises her eyebrows. Outside, the March wind whips tiny ice balls across dirty snowdrifts.

The moose's keen ears twitch as she hears us moving and talking, and she looks down towards the house, a log structure perched on eleven sparsely treed acres. As if taking in the view, she swings her gaze west. Part of a broad valley can be seen where the Telkwa River joins the Bulkley, and with the trees bare, some of the village of Telkwa is visible. Below the moose's hillside, known as Tyhee Mountain, is Tyhee Lake, a frozen oval in the faded countryside. The heavy morning sky dulls but cannot obliterate the rugged peaks of the five mountain ranges that rise startlingly along the valley's western edge.

The moose looks at home in the willow thicket, a favourite feeding spot for her as a calf beside her mother that first winter. Her mother was a scruffy, older moose who had lost her vitality. She moved lethargically, head and shoulders sagging; and her coat, an unhealthy light beige, had huge clumps missing from mange or ticks. The calf did not look healthy either. New calves are gangly and awkward looking, but with her gawky joints this one was an Ichabod Crane look-alike. Angular facial bones gave her a peaky, haunted look. As time went on, she developed unusual behaviours that matched her appearance, making her easy to spot.

From late fall to early spring the first year, we could count on seeing the calf and her mother nearly every day. Though past her prime, the old cow took her maternal duties seriously. Her favourite spot was the open ridge behind the house, where she could keep an eye out for predators and never be more than a few metres from aspen and willow for feeding. She and the calf were inseparable, often in physical contact. I later learned that the strong bond between cow and calf is adaptive; a cow seldom allows her calf to leave her side because it has an innate tendency to heel and will also follow other animals and even people.

Here in northern B.C. we accept that winter's departure is often slow and grudging. The calf's first winter was no exception, with snow flurries that continued into April. Finally, the calf and her mother moved away to their summer range, and the next time we spotted them was in late November. They stuck to the ridge above the house as usual. The cow had no new calf, and the yearling, looking even more uncoordinated with her new growth, followed closely behind her mother as before. The calf's face was lengthening without fleshing out. The mother's coat was even scruffier than before, and she seemed listless. It is not unusual for a yearling to remain with a cow if the cow does not produce a new calf, but there was something both comic and pathetic about this calf's continued close contact with her mother. I doubt the yearling would have survived on her own.

The two browsed our hillside less often the second winter. After a few late winter sightings, we never saw the mother again, and by August the calf was on her own. The abruptness with which a cow moose weans her offspring normally leaves the calf feeling confused and disoriented, but for this weak calf, what followed was close to chaos. Our neighbours began to notice her too. She was on the roadside more often than in the bush. She would gallop down the middle of the road, oblivious to approaching cars, then stop, turn and run back the same way. Sometimes she just stood quietly in driveways or near houses, staring vacantly.

Moose require a lot of space to sustain them, which makes herding impractical. But sometimes after being driven off at calving, yearlings will team up with other young moose. By late September our resident moose, now a spindly two-year-old, was usually seen with a group of three others. She straggled behind as they foraged down by the lake throughout the fall and early winter.

In January temperatures climbed above freezing during the day, which made the road a skating rink at night. I was on my way home after spending too long at the bottom of our road wrestling with tire chains. It was close to full moon, and the road, which gains 150 metres in less than three kilometres, was a glassy ribbon winding up under a bright sky. The moonlight bent through bare aspen and willow, making shadows like craggy witch fingers. The drone of our old Volvo and the predictable clunking and chinging of the tire chains had a hypnotizing effect, and I gripped the wheel, hands still cold from chaining up, thinking of my bed.

Suddenly, off to the right, a dark shape moved up from the ditch into my path. My brain had barely time to register "moose" and hit the brake when the animal spooked, bolted and lost her footing. Legs splayed to the heavens, she tobogganed down the hill right past me, my headlamps spotlighting her flared nostrils and brown eyes bulging in terror. Her crazy carpet ride ended abruptly as she slammed into the snow-plowed mound on the roadside. As she stumbled over an embankment, headed into the field and pulled up to look back, I realized it was our unfortunate moose again. I laughed and chided her right out loud, but my laughter faded quickly when I caught the look in her eyes — such a depth of resigned sadness and maybe even embarrassment. I slipped the car into first gear and chugged up the last two kilometres, wondering whether a moose really feels these emotions.

Throughout the remainder of the winter the moose browsed with two or three others in the upper meadows, then left for her summer range in June. In early September she was back hanging around roadsides and lingering near houses. She looked too gaunt and emaciated to be heading into winter. In late January, while out cross-country skiing with a friend, I spotted the moose feeding at the end of the road. On our way back, nearly an hour later, I noticed she was still standing in the same spot, which seemed unusual. Her left leg was probably already broken.

It has been three days since we spotted the moose through our bathroom window. She seems part of the landscape, the brown-red colours of her coat weaving naturally with the willow shoots. We never see her on her feet. She just lies there with her broken leg tucked under her.

Tonight the moon is waning. It hangs high above the ridge, giving off an eerie light. Around midnight the coyotes start howling, their sudden high-pitched frenzy breaking the stillness. There is a brief silence, and then a different cry, more melodic and lower in pitch, fills the night. Two sharp barks and another howl follow. I jump out of bed and throw open the bedroom door that leads outside. Marc bolts to a sitting position. We wait, not moving or speaking. And then it comes again, long and rich, earthly and otherworldly at the same time. Goose bumps run up my spine and my breath catches sharply.

"Wolves!" I say, still not believing it. Suddenly I need to be closer to the sound. Racing downstairs, flannel nightie flapping, I thrust my bare feet into sloppy bush packs and let myself out the door to the porch. Another call splits the air, this time close beside me — and a pretty dreadful imitation. I watch as Toffee, the golden retriever we are looking after, finishes his chorus. He catches my eye sheepishly, and I chuckle at his attempt to answer the call of the wild. The howling of the wolves, still a long way off, fades, and I go back inside, taking the reluctant retriever with me.

Too excited to sleep, I try not to think about the moose lying in the willows above the house. Instead, I think about the last time we heard the call of the wolves. When we first moved onto our property, we had delays in setting up our sewage system, and one of the fringe benefits of using the outhouse was hearing wolves regularly. It almost made those sub-zero winter treks to the biffy bearable. And we often saw the tracks of six to eight wolves in the snow on the frozen lakes in the logged area at the end of the road.

At that time livestock predation by wolves was being reported not only by local cattlemen but by ranchers throughout the province. As well, guide-outfitters complained of a predator/prey imbalance and lobbied for wolf control legislation. Under pressure from these two groups, a province-wide wolf control program using poison bait was conducted from 1978 to 1984. In the late winter of 1982, Tyhee Mountain became part of the predator control area. No public announcement was made about the baiting, and we learned well after the fact that places we regularly skied with the children had been strewn with strychnine-laden meat. This poison is not selective, and coyotes as well as wolves disappeared from the area for about six years. Without a regular supply of predator leavings to scavenge, the crows and ravens that gossiped on the rails of the compost bin moved on too.

Tonight, I give little thought to the many factors contributing to the slow return of wolves to the area. But I do think long and hard about the propensity of humans to interfere with natural systems.

Not being equipped with a moose's sharp hearing, we are spared the final drama in the backyard that night. Our conversation the following day skirts the topic of wolves and the cow moose, and no one is eager to go up to look for her. But early the next morning, Ingrid shouts from the bathroom window, "Come see the big coyote, Dad! Hurry, it's the biggest coyote I've ever seen!"

The big coyote is a male wolf, his tawny coat reflecting some sparse rays from the early morning sun. His size and obvious strength are impressive. He looks relaxed and well-sated as he stretches. With head up and shoulders arched, he casually scuffs his front feet, then his back feet, lifts his leg and urinates, then rolls playfully beside the willows. After four or five minutes he turns with a flip of his tail and trots up the ridge. As if on cue, a dozen ravens land about fifty metres below the thicket, picking their way towards it. They form only a small part of a steady carrion stream that will continue for nearly two weeks.

The wolf sighting seems to confirm the moose's fate. Our curiosity gets the better of us, and later that day we head up to look at the thicket. The sky is cloudy, but the air has a faint hint of spring. We each take a look at the carcass except for Ingrid, who thinks it is disgusting that we would want to see a dead moose. I am not sure what I expected, but the bare skeleton with a few hide scraps is a shock. It is hard to imagine how an adult moose could be so reduced to this in such a short time.

Ingrid and Paul are matter-of-fact about the wolf getting the moose. Their response seems positive and healthy, though I would have predicted more emotion from them. My own response is a feeling of awe and gratitude at having had the opportunity to watch the moose so closely for so long. Her life still poses many questions. How did she choose our mountain? What was wrong with her? How did she break her leg? These are pieces of her story we'll never know.

A Marmot Meadow

Victoria Miles with Andrew Bryant

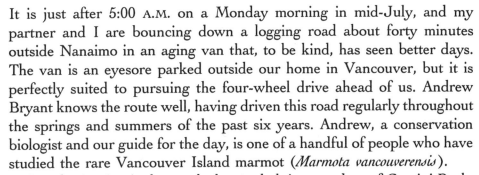

It is just after 5:00 A.M. on a Monday morning in mid-July, and my partner and I are bouncing down a logging road about forty minutes outside Nanaimo in an aging van that, to be kind, has seen better days. The van is an eyesore parked outside our home in Vancouver, but it is perfectly suited to pursuing the four-wheel drive ahead of us. Andrew Bryant knows the route well, having driven this road regularly throughout the springs and summers of the past six years. Andrew, a conservation biologist and our guide for the day, is one of a handful of people who have studied the rare Vancouver Island marmot (*Marmota vancouverensis*).

Our destination is the south slope subalpine meadow of Gemini Peak, part of the Haley Lake Ecological Reserve. The reserve, and the forty square kilometres of mountain and valley that surround it, is home to 75 per cent of all the known colonies of Vancouver Island marmots. We ascend the logging road until the route becomes too narrow to go on safely, then disembark and prepare to complete the steep climb on foot. At this elevation (about a thousand metres above sea level) we are not quite submerged in cloud, and though the sight of the mountains surrounding us is impressive, the dramatic signs of logging activity on the slopes are also in plain view. As we hike, Andrew tells us of the wolves and cougars that are occasional visitors to the area.

Soon we abandon the gravel road and enter a dark forest. The subalpine fir and mountain hemlock are bare of lichen well past the six-foot mark, a sign of the depth of snowdrifts here in winter and of the deer and elk that browse the lichen in their reach for food. As we begin to pick our way across a dewy meadow, it becomes apparent just how few human feet have passed this way. The foot trail created by Andrew in his years of research is barely distinguishable. For a moment I pause, sampling some of the wild strawberries within reach and then experiencing a moment of guilt—perhaps this is not what a visitor to an ecological reserve should be doing. Furtively, I keep the truth of their sweet, delicate flavour to myself.

From the top of the ridge, in the distance, I spy a Vancouver Island marmot. Poised on its hind legs on a massive boulder, nose uplifted in the morning air, the marmot looks around. Marmots, like many species, have monocular eyesight, and they will often peer sideways at their environs. Unperturbed by our presence, the marmot stretches out its four chubby limbs and lies belly-down on the stone. As hibernators, marmots have only five or six months in which to forage for food and gain the fat required to survive the months they will spend in hibernation. Although its Latin name, *Marmota*, means "mountain mouse," this species of rodent can weigh anywhere from 2.5 to 7 kilograms. It does not look as if our first marmot of the day has been wasting any time bulking up. It appears to be well into the process of moulting; dark brown fur is growing in to replace last year's faded, cinnamon-coloured fur.

We situate ourselves among the wildflowers in the meadow to watch for more marmots. Around us are shallow "escape burrows," separate from the main burrow system, which marmots use as temporary havens to avoid predators. The exact structure, size and complexity of the main burrow system for Vancouver Island marmots is still something of a mystery. It is believed that they likely have several tunnels, a nesting pocket and a main hibernating chamber as well as a separate space for urinating and defecating. A lot goes on in the burrow: hibernating, sleeping, avoiding predators, mating, giving birth, nursing the young and escaping the extreme temperatures of the outside world.

These marmots of Gemini are by no means habituated to the presence of humans and this, to me, is a relief. Andrew has worked to minimize his intrusion into marmot habitat, even wearing a special shirt without fail into this meadow in an attempt, however undocumented the success of such a practice might be, to encourage the marmots to recognize him without fear.

For a while, the meadow is empty of marmot life, and we sit and listen to the sounds of thrush and junco that Andrew is able to identify for us. Then with his assistants Ludwig Dyck, a student, and Doug Wahl, a visiting biologist from Australia, Andrew gets to the task at hand, heading over to the burrow entrance that has absorbed much of our attention to set one of the two "Havahart" raccoon traps he has brought. The trapping is done for the purpose of marmot identification and to better understand the process of marmot dispersal. Handling of a marmot is swift, only about three-quarters of an hour from the moment of capture until the animal is released. Andrew has caught just seventy-seven individuals over a six-year period, averaging one marmot for every two to three days of effort. The common practice of setting traps and coming back the next day to check them is made impossible by the fact that marmots can only be kept in the traps for the briefest time; a marmot's body could overheat if forced to endure a warm day above ground. Marmots escape extreme weather conditions and temperatures by going underground to the more stable, moderate temperature of the burrow, which fluctuates with the seasons; it may be about 14° C in midsummer and close to 0° C in late winter. Marmots don't always resort to the burrow when they need to cool off. Unlike most mammals, marmots have no sweat glands; instead they lose heat by conduction, which explains the comical poses they assume when sprawled out on rocks or stumps.

Vancouver Island marmots usually emerge from their burrows between late April and the first few days in May. Food is relatively scarce as deep snow may still cover the meadows around the burrow. So they eat little and travel through the meadow to find patches, bare of snow, where grass has begun to grow. By midsummer, their diet shifts to weeds and flowers, and the marmots may travel shorter distances to forage. A popular spring flower-food for the Gemini Peak colony is spreading phlox. But Vancouver Island marmots are opportunistic in their foraging, eating a wide variety of plants including asters, sweet peas and pearly everlasting. Consistent amongst all colonies is the importance of grasses.

Since most of his field research is conducted in the late spring and summer, when natural food supplies are abundant, Andrew has to provide the marmots with something extraordinarily tempting. It seems that Vancouver Island marmots have a particular preference for peanut butter — the extra-chunky variety. They likely sense its high fat content, a bonus in their quest to gain weight. Peanut butter is smeared on the rocks surrounding the trap, and a great, hopefully irresistible glob is centred inside.

A popular nickname for the alpine marmot is "whistle pig," because of the high, piercing, whistlelike sound it produces when frightened. On this day, the trap nearest to us in the upper meadow has a marmot occupant early on in the waiting game. But we are not forewarned by a whistle; instead, Andrew spots the trap's temporary inhabitant through his binoculars. We all troop over to see who it is.

As it happens, Andrew has seen this female marmot before. She is Oprah on his record books. All the tagged marmots are given names, such as extroverted Oscar and big-bellied Friar Tuck. In one colony, Andrew found three females living together and named them Larry, Moe and Curly. Livewire is aggressive and skittish; Cardinal's coat gave him the appearance of having a red cap on his head, and Luna was the female captured on August 17, 1989, shortly after the lunar eclipse. The names are humorous, but they also speed Andrew's recognition of the animals by enabling him to recall telltale places, dates and characteristic behaviours.

After checking her tag, weight and measurements to calculate growth curves, Andrew lifts the trap door and Oprah shoots out and into the burrow with amazing speed. Later I'll find that the photograph I took in that brief moment shows the burrow entrance — nothing more.

Vancouver Island marmots may live up to nine years, and possibly longer. Oprah is heading for the Vancouver Island record. Andrew believes her to be in her seventh year, tied with Big Guy, Rocky Raccoon and Livewire.

We sink down among the wildflowers once again. Marmot pups, the young of the year, join life above ground for the first time about a month after they are born. Oftentimes the emergence of the litter coincides with Canada Day, July 1. Since we are now two weeks past this date, I had hoped to see pups, but there were none at the Haley Lake colony this year. Usually Vancouver Island marmot pups are born in a litter of three, and they are about forty to forty-five centimetres long (including their tails) when they first greet the great outdoors. In the first few weeks following their surfacing, the marmot pups stay near the burrow entrance and take in only about ten minutes of fresh air at a time. By late July young marmots follow a daily routine similar to that of the adults in the colony: shortly after sunrise they can be seen in the meadow, foraging for food, greeting each other by sniffing necks and touching noses, chirping, tooth chattering, scent marking (adult males will perform this task by urinating or rubbing their cheeks on rocks) and sunning themselves on boulders. The pups are much more playful than the older marmots and spend a lot of time "boxing": standing on their hindquarters, two marmots will push and slap at each other with their forepaws, each one struggling to make the other lose balance in a game that seems to have no end. The game takes on a more serious tone with the adult marmots, becoming a display of dominance and subordination between two colony members.

Playfulness is a common trait among all young marmots; however, a number of factors separate Vancouver Island marmots from their closest mainland relations. They belong to a separate gene pool and are physically distinguished from their marmot cousins by their characteristic chocolate-brown pelage marked with white on the head, chest and around the nose. Recent estimates of their population have concluded that they number between 200 and 300, making them the rarest of the fourteen species of marmot known to exist worldwide. The family life of a Vancouver Island marmot colony is generally characterized by monogamous relationships between adult males and females, though polygamy does occur. Vancouver Island marmots typically live in colonies made up of one adult male, one adult female and small but variable numbers of younger adults, yearlings and pups.

It is past noon in the meadow, and still the chill of early morning clings to the air. The clouds that engulf us separate and reveal the sun sparkling on the lake below, then drift together once again. The air fluctuates from cold to warm to cold again. The occasional marmot comes out of the burrow to settle on a boulder or forage for food near the edge of the meadow. This species probably has never been abundant, though they might have been more common years ago. The most significant limitation to their numbers is the small amount of natural habitat available to them on Vancouver Island. Other natural limits to their population include predation from cougars, golden eagles and wolves, harsh winters and the random deaths of breeding marmots. Although certain colonies have disappeared, given the right conditions they are believed to be able to reactivate an area or colonize elsewhere.

In 1983, a collection of Vancouver Island marmot bones, estimated at 1,500 years old, was discovered at a Port Alberni archaeological site, and other bones have since been found. Marks on these bones indicate that native peoples hunted Vancouver Island marmots, possibly for food and clothing.

The Vancouver Island marmot is officially listed as an endangered species by the Committee on the Status of Endangered Wildlife in Canada and the B.C. Ministry of Environment, and it is protected by law from hunting or collection under the province's Wildlife Act. The Vancouver Island Marmot Recovery Team, made up of biologists as well as officials from federal and provincial wildlife agencies, forest companies and conservation organizations, was established in 1988. This team produced a recovery plan for the marmot, the eventual goal being to boost the species' numbers.

Understanding the process of dispersal, in which some young adult members of the colony travel down their home mountain, through forest, around lakes and up over neighbouring slopes, is essential to the health and future of the entire species. Today, marmot dispersal is complicated by the altered states of logged-over areas. Survival rates seem to be higher in natural colonies than in logging slash, but this can't yet be confirmed. Still, in a natural colony, females have a 38-per-cent chance of living to age four and thus achieving sexual maturity; in clearcut, the equivalent statistic is a sobering 16 per cent. Habitat protection is an essential factor to the future of the species. The Ministry of Environment has pledged that habitat acquisition for the benefit of the marmot will continue on Vancouver Island. Already, 127 hectares of land set aside by the logging companies MacMillan Bloedel and Fletcher Challenge comprise the Haley Lake Ecological Reserve. In 1991, 300 hectares on Green Mountain, home to another colony, were designated as a critical wildlife management area, and Strathcona Provincial Park may also be able to provide a safe haven for colonies in the future.

Marmots are characteristically early to bed and early to rise, and so we find ourselves done for the day just after 3:00 P.M. As we descend Gemini, I allow myself to indulge in a belief that this place, and its inhabitants, will exist at least as long again as the ten thousand years that have passed since glaciers pulled away the rock face and made the marmots' meadow.

The Power in Wild Things
Neall Calvert

There is a power in creatures in the wild to move me, to affect my thinking patterns, even to heal me. I've been watching this effect for several years. My encounters with creatures seem to involve some barely explainable mystery that speaks to a deep nurturing only (Mother) Nature can provide.

One summer day, caught in depression and despair, I trudged under a high blue sky along a dyke of the Alouette River. On one side of me in the blueberry bushes, an air cannon boomed randomly to scare off hungry birds. Across the river, tranquil fields and farmhouses demonstrated a way of life far from the purposelessness I felt inside. After more than an hour of listening to my feet scuff the gravel path, something caused me to look up. At first I saw only a bird. Then I looked again and saw the broad-winged eagle approaching from the north. I continued gazing as with majestic wingstrokes it described a large circle over my head. Then it headed back from where it had come.

In those few moments, something inside me changed. My dark mood lifted. It seemed that some wordless message had been delivered. As some inner destination seemed to have been reached, I turned to walk back.

Another day, another walk — this time on Galiano Island through forest trails to the lighthouse at the northern tip, Dionisio Point. In the fast-flowing channel off the point, there unfolded before me a small scene of complete chaos: grey and white sea birds, perhaps a species of small sea gull, alternately hovered and landed in the water. In the air, they flapped their wings madly; in the swirling waters, they paddled equally boisterously. They didn't appear to be feeding. Two or three at a time would lift off, then land, then others would repeat the noisy flapping and paddling cycle. After a few minutes, something inside me suggested that they were playing. This thought nourished me. I wondered at how driven I felt, how hard I worked for not very large rewards. These birds seemed to know something I didn't.

Later that year, I was driving out of the city to visit my elderly parents, from whom I was estranged for years. I knew that my father was dying and that the visit might not be a comfortable one. On the way, I spotted an eagle sitting high in a leafless tree, and immediately I sensed the visit would go all right.

In August of this year, on a hot day after weeks of sunshine, the air outside was shimmering and thick, and, heeding the urgings of the boy within me, I got up from my freelance editing work to roam the back fields of a south Langley hobby farm. An afternoon like this seemed rare, and two hours of close attention to a technical manual had earned me a change of pace.

We started out across the small field, my inner boy and I, passed the barn and negotiated the gate into the six-acre field I had cut with the neighbour's tractor a month before. The grass hadn't grown much since there had been little rain. A barbed-wire fence spans the back of the field, and from there the property slopes sharply down to Upper Campbell Creek, in this season a shrub-filled mudflat.

I strolled down the trail that angles across the slope, saluted by birches and cottonwoods on either side. Once at the bottom, I glanced up at the hillside, covered in pale-gold high grass that hadn't seen a tractor for years, if ever. I realized that although I had been at the bottom of the meadow near the creek several times, I had never looked down from the top.

From up there, amidst the pure grass and warm sunshine, I gazed at the little bowl below me. Dark evergreens partially shielded the creek. Buzzing insects crisscrossed the air nonchalantly — dragonflies! Like tiny biplanes they buzzed back and forth across the little meadow. This day was true summer. I stood and let it fill me up right to the brim. I returned slowly to the house.

A few hours later I was outside sunbathing when a familiar buzzing sound interrupted my dozing. A dragonfly careered across the space between me and the raspberry canes in the garden. I stood up and it stayed in the vicinity, flying twenty-foot vertical loops and then hovering at eye level, its glistening turquoise body competing with the blue sky above. But each time it completed a loop it would stop several feet closer to me. Ten feet...eight feet...six feet...four feet. How near would it come?

Once, as if to demonstrate some particular bit of dragonfly acrobatics, at top speed it jauntily dipped its tail forward beneath its body. Quite a show. I felt dazzled, elated. All too soon it was over. I started to think about what I had just witnessed. Unbelievable as it sounds, I sensed that something unusual and mysterious had happened at the meadow a few hours earlier. I had been noticed! While I had been watching the dragonflies, they had also been watching me. The acrobat had come on a return visit, as if to complete some wordless contract written in the hot summer air.

I ignore Nature at my peril, I've realized over the past few years. Without the context of its greater intelligence, any work I do is meaningless, and thus depressing. I must include Nature in the equation of my life because — whether it takes the form of a solitary eagle, a flock of sea birds or even the cloud formations that pass over the city almost every day — it is evidence of something larger at work, something that has the power to enliven and to heal individual women and men.

Heroic Measures

Mary C. Foster

One fall, when I was reading in the sun porch, I kept hearing a scratching outside. I ignored it for some time, then suddenly realized that there was probably a squirrel in the water barrel. The previous year, when emptying the barrel before winter, we had found a dead baby squirrel.

Putting on gardening gloves, I took off the lid, and sure enough, there was a squirrel, paddling for dear life and trying to climb up the side. I picked him out, and he immediately went like a wet noodle, absolutely done for and apparently dead.

I took him into the house and examined him closely. I marvelled at his tiny paws and sharp claws, his exquisite little nose and mouth and shapely ears. He was not dead, but his breathing was a deep shudder with many seconds between breaths. Remembering that it was not wise to try heroic methods to resuscitate wild creatures, I decided to put him on the garage roof, hoping that his relatives would come to his aid. (We had had squirrels living in our garage for seventeen years.) One hour later, he was still there, alone and quite cold, so I put him in an old birdcage, in a nest of deep sheepskin.

Half an hour later, there appeared to be no improvement in my little patient, whom I now diagnosed as suffering from hypothermia. I decided that the best thing I could do for him was to put him inside my shirt next to my skin, so with him cradled around my waist, I sat down to watch TV. It was almost an hour before I felt him stirring and moving about, and it was then I realized the enormity of what I had done. Peering cross-eyed down the open neck of my shirt, I was transfixed to see his head poking out, just a few inches from my nose. I held my breath in fright. Then the unbelievable happened: he rubbed his left ear with his left paw, and right ear with his right paw, and disappeared inside again. I guess he felt warm and comfortable. Fifteen minutes later, he really began to move, pulling himself round my midriff with those needle-sharp claws.

I decided that it was time for him to go, but how to get rid of him? I went into the garage, knelt on the floor and tried to shuck him out of my shirt, but he clung on. At this point, my husband came down the drive, and seeing me kneeling, asked if I was saying my prayers.

"Go away," I hissed, "I've got a squirrel in my shirt."

He leaned closer. "*What* did you say?"

I repeated my remark, whereupon, looking startled, he left to watch me through the window. More flapping of my shirt did not dislodge the occupant, so I just kept kneeling, waiting for him to come out in his own time. Eventually, he clawed his way up my back (ouch!), crawled out my shirt collar, jumped onto the workbench, ran along to the end, climbed up the wall and disappeared into the nest area without a backward glance.

The Visitor

Elizabeth Thunstrom

There was a loud SMACK! sound from the bathroom followed by a lot of splashing. Bathtime was over for the newest member of the household. Usually babies are carefully supervised during a bath, but this one preferred hers alone, with the shower doors firmly closed. She looked different, too. Her body was totally covered with shiny brown fur and ended in a broad, flat tail. Her back feet were webbed, with one claw on each foot modified into her own personal comb; her dark-brown eyes looked warily around and her small ears were pressed close to her head. She had four large, orange-coloured teeth. Our baby was, in fact, a young beaver!

As a wildlife rehabilitator, I have had an unusual assortment of critters spend time under my roof. Beave, as we called her, had been orphaned when the family home was dynamited. Somehow she had survived, to be found dirty and stunned on the riverbank.

Beavers have close family bonds; babies live with their parents and last year's young, who assist in their care. They are born fully furred and with the eyes open, and start to eat solid food soon after birth, although they are not fully weaned until about eight weeks. We believed Beave was about nine or ten weeks old when she was brought in. She was initially set up in a special cage with a small pool, but she refused to eat and buried her head in the corner, making small whimpering sounds. An unusual feature of beavers is that when frightened or under stress, drops of liquid ooze from their eyes, looking like tears. Beave looked as sad as she undoubtedly felt without her family close to her.

It was decided to set up a special home for her, and at this point she came to live with my family. It is illegal to keep wildlife without a permit. Rehabilitators are trained to care for injured and orphaned wildlings in such a way that they will be able to return to their own environment as soon as possible; it was important that we do our best to provide for Beave's needs in such a way that she would remain wild and not become dependent on humans. First we had to get her to eat. A large wooden pen was constructed in the basement; one corner held a platform of crisscrossed sticks and a heating pad under a tented blanket as a substitute for the lodge. A trip to Value Village produced a stuffed toy beaver the same size as the real animal. This was put into the "lodge" too. Beave immediately snuggled up to the warm furry toy and, with a deep sigh, fell asleep.

We surrounded the platform with chunks of apple and tasty lengths of willow branches, and by the next morning, we were pleased to see that she had nibbled at the food.

A pan of water was placed in the pen; it is very important for beavers that they keep their fur clean, and they also need water for bathroom purposes. In addition, as Beave grew stronger, she needed to be able to swim for exercise, so twice a day the bathtub was filled and she dived and cavorted behind the shower doors. It was rather difficult if we needed the facilities too; the worst day was when we had houseguests and we all had to get ready to go to a wedding in between Beave's bathtimes!

It really got her excited when the plug was pulled; it seemed to trigger some instinct that indicated "Danger! Water levels are dropping!" At that point she would slap the water very sharply with her tail, just as the adults do in the wild. It didn't do a lot for the state of the bathroom floor. Once the water had drained out of the tub, she would sit up on her hind legs and squeeze the moisture out of her fur with her forepaws, which resemble hands and are very dexterous. Following this, she would use the toothed claws on her hind feet to comb all the fur until it was quite dry. At first Beave tumbled over when she tried to sit upright, but each day she became more confident. I had to pick her up in a towel to return her to her pen; she didn't like to be held, yet she tolerated it and never bit me.

Finally the day came when she graduated to a large outdoor pen with a proper pool. She now weighed well over fifteen pounds and was strong, swam well for long periods and, best of all, did not attempt to come to us. It was time for her to go. With guidance from the Wildlife Branch of the provincial government (they are responsible for native mammals and birds of prey), a suitable site was found where Beave would be safe from traps and adult beavers while she grew to maturity. She nosed out of the transport carrier and looked all around. Then, in one smooth movement, she slid into the water and dived. We held our collective breath. Would she be okay? A sleek dark head broke the surface briefly, then dived again; each time she stayed under a little longer and travelled farther, until she disappeared in the distance. I wished her a good life and a mate and family of her own.

A Grizzly Encounter
Steven Waʃylik

The grizzly bear has been a symbol of wilderness for as long as anyone can remember. The conservation officers in B.C. have had a love/hate relationship with this charismatic animal since the first days of the C.O. Service. While stationed as the district conservation officer in Mackenzie, B.C., I was to carry on this relationship in its truest tradition.

The old-timers of the trapping and guiding fraternities told me that the area around Mackenzie has always been known as grizzly country. "You could plan on having one of those buggers trying to wrap his arms around you every time you camped near here in the old days," someone said.

It was inevitable that I was going to have a face-to-face meeting with a grizzly. But, being a believer in fate, I decided to let it happen rather than go looking for the opportunity.

I was working with RCMP Constable Glen Pelly late one summer evening. We had been checking the local area for ever-elusive poachers but had only managed to come up with a couple of kids conducting a biology experiment on a side road near town. Then our radio dispatcher called and advised that someone had just hit a bear on the highway south of town, near the garbage dump road. The caller wasn't sure if the bear was dead or not. Another RCMP member was patrolling near the area and said he'd go have a look. Over the radio I cautioned him that there had been three grizzlies, a sow and a pair of three-year-old cubs, near the accident site earlier in the day, in addition to the two dozen or so grizzlies resident in the dump.

It wasn't very long before the officer called us back and said that there was a dead bear cub in the ditch. He couldn't tell me whether it was a grizzly or not, but he said the two standing beside it sure were. Ever conscious of my responsibility to try to keep Mother Nature's creatures from coming in direct contact with Detroit's motorized machines, Glen and I decided that we had better go and have a look.

It was dark by that time, and we had two live bears, a dead one and, nearby, at least a couple dozen more. Neither of us had ever done much work with a sow grizzly that had just lost a cub. At best, mother grizzlies with their cubs can be mean, so we figured that this sow would be idling at mean and ready to gear up from there.

Unknown to the grizzlies, we had an ace in the hole: my German shepherd, Max. He and I had dealt with several bears since I'd rescued him from the pound a few years before. We had a good system worked out: he was always to be between me and the bear.

Max had a keen ability to sense when a bear was around. The week before, we had worked on tracking a black bear that had been hit by a car. The bear had gone into some dense brush somewhere near the highway. By using Max to track the injured bear, I had been able to keep both my eyes open to look around us. I knew that we were getting close when Max started to growl. This growl is very quiet and comes from deep in his chest. His tail was curled up over his back and he was looking straight ahead. Sure enough, just visible a few feet away, was the injured bear. I had learned through experience to trust Max whenever I was looking for a bear, and I rarely would go to a bear complaint without him.

On our way out to the site, we met the other officer returning to town. He told us he had last seen the two live bears on the opposite side of the road from the dead one. When we arrived, the other bears were nowhere to be seen. This should have been good news, but it was too dark to see much anyway. We determined that the bear in the ditch was one of the two sub-adult grizzly cubs that had been frequenting the area with the sow for some time. The cubs were three years old and weighed over two hundred pounds each. Their mother was even bigger. This meant that out in the dark somewhere were at least two grizzlies capable of rendering myself and Glen to bear shit in an instant.

Glen and I decided to remove the dead bear so that the other two wouldn't hang around the highway and possibly get hit themselves. How to do it was the problem. Max was running laps around the back of the truck, excited about the proximity of the bears. I imagine he was also excited about the prospect of one or all of us going in one end of a grizzly and out the other. After turning on the truck's side and rear spotlights, arming Glen with a flashlight and a shotgun, and briefly discussing who was going to do what if Mom showed up, Glen and I left the truck. I let Max out but told him to stick around; he immediately went down into the ditch and confronted the bear. Once he had confirmed that the bear was dead, he came back and lay down near the truck. With Glen patrolling the road and shouting encouragement, I hooked up ropes and snatch-blocks, and we eventually got the dead bear into the truck.

This is where technology started to let us down: all the auxiliary lights on the truck went out. We were left with the headlights only. I got my flashlight out and had a good look around. No bears. I got Max to sit just behind the truck as a rear guard. He wasn't impressed at the thought of being a canine sacrifice to a grizzly, but at least I knew where he was, and it was less likely that Glen or I would mistake him for a bear in the dark and put a hole in him. About this time the ropes got all tangled up in the snatch-block. Now, I have trouble undoing my boots in the dark, so trying to untie a knot that would have kept a whole Boy Scout troop busy was more than my meagre supply of patience could handle. I had just thrown down the tangle of rope and pulleys when Max started to growl. Thinking he was getting impatient, I told him to shut up. To his credit, he didn't. I grabbed the flashlight and shone it at him and was just about to give him a lecture when I realized he was growling from way down deep and staring out into the night. That's when I saw the grizzly sow coming up out of the ditch.

Things started to happen rather quickly, especially my getting into the box of the truck. I knew if we didn't act fast I'd be sharing the box with the grieving mother very soon. I yelled something at Glen; I can't remember what it was, but he thinks I said, "There'sthesowshootthe-goddamnthingquick." He said later he couldn't understand me very well because his ears can't pick out words at such a high octave.

All hell broke loose. Max took off past the bear into the night. I shone my flashlight after him and saw that he was chasing the remaining cub. I fired a shot near the sow with my handgun. She stopped and stood her ground on the other side of the very narrow truck box. By this time Glen was around the front of the truck, and he fired a shot towards the cub. Max decided that he was likely going to be hit by friendly fire and decided to come back. I don't know when Max realized that the sow was in front of him, but it was most likely when he was about two feet from her hindquarters. As Max stopped directly behind the sow and started to growl, Glen fired another shot after the cub, which took off into the bush. Mom started to think it might be a good idea to pay her last respects some other time. Glen and I both encouraged her with another shot. The last time I saw her, she and the cub were heading up into the trees, and both bears soon disappeared into the night.

It took a minute for the gunsmoke to clear and the nerves to settle down. "Did you hit her?" I asked Glen. "No," he replied. "Did you?" I knew that even given an appropriate amount of time, steady nerves, good weather and lots of light, I would have trouble hitting a charging bear with a handgun. A quick check showed that Max had four legs and wasn't leaking any vital fluids.

Having had enough excitement for one night, we left and went to my house. As the night wore on and Captain Morgan's rum steadied our nerves, the bear got closer, and moved faster, and the night got much darker. But despite all our exaggeration the three of us knew we had come very close to seeing just how mad a grizzly can get.

Max's bear-tracking days are all but over now as he's lost an eye, is going deaf and has a heart murmur. But he still comes to work with me every day, and on the occasions when I need him, his quiet growl, coming from deep in his chest, still tells me there's a bear nearby.

And the Biologist Said I Was Lucky!
Jacqueline Ward

Twenty-four hours after the fact, the experience seems surreal. An adrenalin-produced feeling of exhilaration still makes me shake my head and wonder if the whole thing ever happened. (Is that a nervous giggle I feel again in the back of my throat?)

The brightness was beginning to fade from the afternoon as dusk approached. Evening chores were done, and I headed back from the barn shortly before six o'clock. The little dogs, Tess and Bandie, raced ahead of me, and Rocky, our Saint Bernard/malamute, was already waiting for us in the driveway in front of the house. He was barking urgently and bounding back and forth. As I approached, he ran up the driveway, urging me and the smaller dogs to follow. Probably chasing the stray cat, I thought. One of their favourite games.

It took only seconds to realize the fuss was not about a cat. As we rounded a slight curve in the drive, we were face to face with a pack of at least eight wolves. Four of them hightailed it back to the edge of the bush, and I counted at least another four that remained to challenge us. Bandie, a springer spaniel, had already lost her dad and brother to wolves and was not inclined to stick around. She raced, scrambling frantically over the lumber pile, for the safety of the house. The pursuing wolf turned his attention to the easier prey of the remaining dogs. I couldn't believe what was happening!

Tess thinks herself to be the farm cop. Her self-appointed job is to scare off every wandering visitor by barking and making aggressive advances without actually fighting. These wolves needed driving away, and so again and again she barked, rushed and retreated to my side. I'm not sure what became of the four wolves who leaped away when I originally surprised them. Whether they returned to form part of the confusion or whether they remained at a distance, I don't know. My immediate attention was focussed on my dogs.

The wolves weren't leaving. I had no time to go back for a gun (would I even have known how to use it?) and helplessly threw a chunk of wood at the wolf closest to Rocky, distracting him only slightly. I had no other weapons. At some point in this melee, I started screaming, non-stop, arm-waving screaming. Perhaps the result was some confusion on their part, for the wolves did not actually attack in force. Instead, the one who was after Rocky lunged in to bite at the dog's back legs, then stood back when I screamed and rushed him.

My dogs are my children. The wrenching heartbreak of losing two to wolves was buried only a shallow distance from the surface. It flooded upward and drove all reason from me. When the wolf closed in again, I ran up and kicked him on the right hindquarter. He was surprised enough to back off momentarily but quickly regained confidence and moved in again. Repeatedly I screamed and kicked out at him, sometimes making contact but more often just aiming in his general direction, then leaping backwards.

Amidst it all, like a film stilled on a single frame, I was aware of the wolf's beauty — the thick coat of rich, dense blends of browns and blacks, the tail bushy and erect. He had six to eight inches on my Saint Bernard at the shoulders, with long legs and almond slanted eyes. Since he was obviously the most aggressive, I imagine he was the dominant male. The others seemed content to keep behind him.

Finally Rocky made enough retreating progress that I was able to stand between the two animals and urge the dog to head for home. Tess followed, and with me continuing to scream and run backwards down the drive, we started home. Rocky's wolf followed tentatively. When I got close enough to the house to turn and run, he didn't follow further.

With Tess, Rocky and Bandie secured inside, I called a neighbour. Howling and yipping from the angry, frustrated pack filled the air and was heard by other neighbours a quarter of a mile away. By the time help arrived, the wolves were gone.

It's over this time. They have left to find other pickings. The adrenalin rush of last night has subsided into a feeling of incredulity. I can't believe they didn't care that I was there. I can't believe they didn't make an all-out attack on the dogs. But most of all, I can't believe I went charging wildly and unarmed into a pack of wolves.

A numbness sporadically takes hold of my thoughts, and a fist fills my stomach with an aching knot. "You're lucky," a biologist told me. "Not many people have even seen a wolf, let alone an entire pack."

It's not over. This is just the middle of the story. To date we have suffered the loss of two dogs. Wolves chased the dogs right up onto the porch one morning, knocking Rocky's back legs out from under him repeatedly as he raced for safety. That time my husband was on the porch yelling, and they stopped their pursuit twenty-seven feet from the house. One afternoon three weeks ago, a lone wolf stood boldly in the drive eyeing the calves. Hearing the serenades of a howling pack is no longer a novelty. Time of day and time of year make no difference. Sounds like the wilderness? We live seven miles from the tourist town of Qualicum Beach, one mile from the island highway.

For years I comfortably believed the wolf/dog cross theory. But personal experience has a way of shedding a different light on theory. These are unmistakably timber wolves. Sheep, dogs and cattle are much easier prey than the numerous deer that fill our woods.

Both my husband and I are animal sympathizers, whether wild or domestic. I find it very difficult to reconcile my conservationist views with the reality of our situation. Somehow it was so easy to believe and teach the mystique of the misunderstood wolf before the events of the past few years. Human habitation is encroaching on their domain. They are fighting back. It's a very real problem, and a lot of soul-searching must accompany any attempted solution.

Evolution in Every Direction
Brian Brett

The ribs of the dead trees broke against the sky above the spit, and vast cumulus clouds raced the sun to the horizon. We launched the boat, my father and I, and steered into the sky just beyond the spit. The big water was quiet, slow despite the life that flashed beneath us, out of sight and hungry.

Rebecca Spit. Not many had discovered it then. We camped alone by the sandy beach, stuffing ourselves with clams, oysters and the huckleberries that grew in the deep wood. But most of all, we came for the bluebacks, those small coho salmon that rushed the waters of the strait every June. They travelled in huge schools, fins boiling the water when they surfaced.

Throughout the week we trolled under sunrise and sunset skies; then the dogfish arrived, seeping into the bay overnight, and our lines fought only these small sharks. They took bait, they took Tom Macks, they even took Flashtails on the surface. We fished shallow for the cohos, with four ounces of lead, sometimes less. If we felt lucky we'd shift deep and try for spring salmon, but there wasn't a chance with the dogfish striking. Our fishing turned into carnage as we destroyed whatever we caught. Once, we hooked a coho and a dogfish came up behind, leaving us only a head attached to the hook.

My father hated these deep pests...mudsharks...dogfish... They stripped your bait, bent your hooks, snapped your lines, devoured, scoured the ocean bottom like quick vacuums with teeth. Everything has its place, but some things have no place with fishermen, especially dogfish. There was a war here, and we lost. Twenty years ago the ocean was endless.

It was a killing day. I'd bludgeoned and slit open too many sharks, dumping the entrails over the side, watching the carnivores, still alive, devour their own guts. They are difficult to kill; a simple blow is never enough.

At last the mountains covered the sun and my cursing father steered the boat back to camp. No salmon lay at our feet, only one giant shark that we hadn't bothered to slit and return to the sea. Exhausted by the day's murders, we beached as the last red followed the sun into darkness. A big hook dragged the night over our heads, and the moon followed like one of those slow sharks looking for the rip. The broken trees at the spit's end, funereal, cast an eeriness, reminding me of Indian graveyards and the strange fears that follow men into forests.

My disgusted father limped up the beach, stiff and angry, leaving me the bloodied skiff. I flipped out the five-foot shark and used sea water to wash away the gore in the boat. Tomorrow, we'd try again.

Sometimes we break our patterns. I had slit and hurled two dozen sharks into the sea during the past few days, always by the tail, avoiding the sharp spike in the dorsal fin. This one I grabbed by the midsection and lifted off the sand to wheel it around and into the sea, but I squeezed. My hands became someone else's hands, sensitive to the life. Something came out with a gentle pop, and it was alive — a shark from the belly of the shark. I dropped the dead mother and stared at the small replica squirming in the sand.

I picked up the shark. Dirty and almost dead it wriggled in my hand, yolk sac still attached. Then I slid the shark into the shallows where it lay quiet for a moment; it shivered and swam a short, slow distance before it turned and settled to the bottom, watching me — cold blooded, accusing. Only five inches long and already aware of where it belonged, what its life was. I returned to the corpse of the mother. When I'd finished milking her womb, six of the sharks swam the shallows, their tiny eyes glowing like emerald pins in the moonlight; they were looking for the great sea stretch ahead. Then they were gone. I hurled the carcass of the mother after them; perhaps she'd be their first meal.

At camp, I said nothing as I sat down to a dinner of yesterday's salmon stuffed with huckleberries and baked over the fire. The night was good. The moon poured its silver on us; we were unearthly figures by the fire, throwbacks, savages from another time devouring the flesh of the sea. And I was wilder than any. Something deep had been driven into me, had gaffed my bloodstream. I'd taken innocent life, and given a bit of it back. My brain was more simple, swam on a stem of streamlined, uncomplicated nerves. My teeth were longer and sharper when they sank into the meat of the salmon. I was cartilage instead of bone. My hand, evolved from a finny protuberance by centuries of mutation, seemed strange; and I knew my green eyes glowed in the dark. I'd become wilder than any of us; I was the sorcerer, the land-walking belly-slitting father of the sharks.

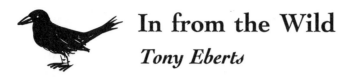

In from the Wild
Tony Eberts

While my father was very careful to shoot only buck deer out of season — and then only when the weather was cool enough to keep the meat from spoiling before it could be eaten or preserved — not all the residents of Adams Lake were so particular. Sometimes there were gun-happy hotshots from Outside who would come up the lake in a rented boat and fire at virtually anything they saw along the shore. Once we almost lost a dog to one of these jerks. My pointer-spaniel cross named Danny ran out onto the beach as we walked a shoreside trail and drew a shot. I had heard the outboard motor and glimpsed the boat, and at the sound of the shot I ran out onto the beach, shouting, and the two men in the boat revved up the motor and drew out from shore, carefully looking away from me.

Early one summer my sister and I came upon the carcass of a doe lying on that same beach, dead from a bullet through her lungs, and back in some low bushes we found a spotted fawn, all spindly legs and ears and eyes. Instinct had kept it lying quietly in cover, but it showed no fear of us and we picked it up and brought it home in a lather of emotions. We were outraged at the wanton, wasteful killing of the little creature's mother, but we were overjoyed at being able to save the fawn and to have its endearing, fragile beauty actually in our hands and in our lives. By the time we got the fawn home, we had already treated its future in an almost practical way and had hit upon a means of avoiding the awful possibility of Father potting our pet when it was full grown and back in the wilds: we would find a way to transport it across the lake and release it where Father never hunted.

In the meantime, Father helped us build a pen for the fawn out of leftover chicken wire and scrap lumber, complete with a snug little house with a nest of soft hay. Mother rigged up a nursing bottle using the smallest finger of an old rubber glove as a nipple, and we fed the hungry creature warm milk with corn syrup added. It was a male, so we rather prosaically named him Bucky. In the first few days his strength increased remarkably, and his charm with it. He was fearless, touching noses with the dogs, moving with only the occasional stumble over the grass on incredibly dainty cloven hoofs and melting all hearts with his huge, dark eyes. But after a couple of weeks, Bucky seemed to weaken a little, and though his appetite persisted he moved more slowly. Frantically we tried to hit upon a feeding formula that would perk him up. We tried switching from fresh milk to the canned, condensed kind, and additives included cod liver oil, honey, even a strong tea made from the buck-brush older deer browse on. Nothing worked. There are, of course, special substances in a doe's milk that provide particular nourishment and immunities, and there were no substitutes that we could offer. The little deer dwindled, day by day, and even his death was graceful; Sally and I were on the edge of being persuaded that the right thing was to end Bucky's quiet suffering when he simply lay down, went to sleep and died.

Nothing that irresistibly appealing should have to die, and we were sharply stung by the unfairness of it. Even Father, the harvester of venison on the hoof, was saddened. It took the arrival of Edgar Allan Poe to snap us out of a prolonged period of mourning.

Edgar Allan was an unlucky member of a small flock (or "murder") of crows that decided to harass a red-tailed hawk. The hawk was perched, almost out of sight, near the top of a big cottonwood, and the crows assailed the big bird with great noise and swoopings. Eventually it flew, and inevitably the crows began behaving like fighter aircraft attacking a bomber, diving down and looping under the hawk, sometimes coming almost close enough to touch it. Edgar got a little too close to the bomber's undercarriage, and before he knew what was happening his wing tip had been gripped and mangled by well-armed talons. We watched the whole drama, and saw the crow come spiralling down to earth like a small, sun-blackened Icarus.

The crow was damaged and stunned. It hid in some tall grass and wasn't located until Punch, my father's little springer spaniel, sniffed it down and retrieved it. Punch's gentle mouth was legendary at our place, for he once carried a blown-glass Christmas tree ornament around for an hour without damaging it. The bird, in fact, was beginning to draw blood on the dog's nose before we got them apart. In the tussle the wing tip came away neatly, and we staunched the bleeding with a cold compress and then applied Mercurochrome and a bandage. Again, Father went to work with small boards and chicken wire and made a cage about six feet cubical while Sally and I kept the crow in a cardboard box and fed it cold fried potatoes. We soon learned its eating habits: it would eat anything, and try to eat everything.

It was a crow and not a raven, but Father had recently read us the famous poem, so it was decided the blue-black bird was close enough. Edgar Allan Poe never learned to say "Nevermore," but he had a splendid repertoire of cawings and croakings and some wordlike noises and, for a fowl, a foul temper. He always tried to take the fingers along with the offering, and would clack and snap his heavy beak and sidle along his perch to get within striking distance. It was clear that he would never fly again, which gave him no chance to survive in the wild, so Edgar was condemned to life behind bars and we were sentenced to look after him. And after we got used to avoiding his beak, we actually began to enjoy the little beast's company. He had a way of hopping up and down on his perch when he saw us coming (for the summer his cage was kept under the roof of an open hay shed). Cynically, we assumed that it was only the prospect of something to eat that sparked this miming of joy, but it soon became clear that he would do it even when we approached empty-handed, and often continued the dance while we talked to him. Occasionally other crows came by and he would holler at them; they would yell back, and sometimes a free bird would land on a rail close by and indulge in a squawking match with the prisoner, who seemed more angry than pleased to see one of his fellows. When the visitor went away, Edgar Allan never threw himself against the chicken wire in an effort to follow. More often than not he would shrug his shoulders and take a nap.

He swore horribly at the dogs, and they usually kept out of his space. We put marbles and broken tin soldiers and odds and ends in his cage, and he would play with them, shifting them around and seeming, like a magpie, to favour the brighter and shinier objects. The bottom of the cage was wire, too, and the structure stood on a wooden platform. We put a thin layer of sand over the bottom, and when the dirt built up we would simply hoist the cage, sweep off the platform, replace the cage and add a new layer of sand. He competed with the pigs for kitchen leftovers, and we also gave him handfuls of dandelion greens and alfalfa. Rotten-hearted nest robber that he was, his favourite treat was an egg from one of the few bantam hens; he would tap it open and slurp up the contents with every sign of contentment. I remember waiting for him to wink or belch when the egg was gone, but he only stropped his beak on his perch.

The most notable of the wild creatures that we shared our place with (Father explained that we shouldn't call them pets because they were not; they were wild beings that lived captive lives with us and lost their natural fear of people) was a miniature black bear. It was not a cub. It was a dwarf of a bear that came sniffing around the chicken run one day when my father was away on his trapline, and it frightened us because, at a distance, it was hard to know how small it was. I loaded the .30-30 and took it along when we locked the dogs in the house and went to investigate.

When we discovered that the beast was not at all afraid of us, and that it was no bigger than a large English bulldog, we assumed it was a cub only a few months old. But there was none of the baby cuteness of a cub; its claws were long and rather weathered, the nose was also long, and bony. Still, it was the size of the cub, and one of the prime safety rules of the bush is to avoid bear cubs assiduously. Getting between a cub and its mother was considered about as foolhardy as playing Russian roulette with a double-barrelled shotgun. So, under Mother's orders, we walked away from the little bear while it stood and watched us, and we went back in the house to see if the animal would go away or be joined by a she-bear. There was no sign of another animal, and our visitor shinnied up an apple tree after the small amount of fruit still on the branches. We were in a serious quandary. This wasn't some cute little creature that could be caged and fed; and, on the loose, it posed a threat to the orchard, the chickens and perhaps the dogs as well. It was a walking mystery, too, with its total lack of fear. That was when we thought again of the old plan about the deer — Adams Lake as a barrier. Father was a practical man who would find little merit in trying to live with a bear, even if it was a small one. Father would be back from his trapline in two days. We must act, and time was of the essence.

Mother had serious doubts about the enterprise, but her soft heart and sense of adventure brought her into it. The idea was to simply throw a strong canvas tarp over the animal, bundle it up tightly, pop it in the spare rowboat and have it across the lake in a jiffy (less than two miles, at a rowing speed of five miles per hour, would do the job in about twenty minutes). The scheme started out even better than we expected when the bear actually walked onto the middle of the tarpaulin after an apple and we simply threw the ends and sides over him and had the bundle tied with a rope before he started to make a strong fuss. The animal was heavier than we figured, though, at an estimated seventy-odd pounds, and we had to drag him to shore and heave him into the small boat with the aid of fear-driven adrenalin. We hadn't gone more than fifty yards, with Mother pulling strongly at the oars, before a set of wicked claws ripped a six-inch gash in the heavy canvas. We shrieked in unison when the claws were withdrawn and a muzzle full of remarkably long teeth took their place. "Roll him over," Mother cried. "Keep away from all the teeth and things, but roll him over."

And so we travelled across the lake, the oars going at an incredible rate and my sister and I grabbing folds of tarp at the rear of the bear and standing the poor beast on its head each time it righted itself and began another rip in the canvas. Thoughts of the havoc that would occur in a rowboat crewed by a woman, two children and a small but angry bear kept us working tirelessly. Still, by the time Mother drove the boat onto the far shore, the bear was restrained by little more than a sort of harness of frayed cloth. Its head, complete with red-glinting eyes and gnashing teeth, plus at least three legs, were free. We jumped out of the boat and pelted down the beach while our passenger, no longer kept off balance, quickly shredded the last of the tarpaulin and leaped onto the sand. About two hundred yards away, we stopped and stared at the bear, and the bear stared back. Then it shook itself, snorted, ran up into the trees and vanished. If high fives had been invented then, we would have used them to congratulate ourselves. But Sally and I were sworn to secrecy about the whole affair, and years passed before Father discovered the answer to the mystery of the disappearing tarpaulin and the strange, deep scratches on the floorboards of the boat.

The Wolf and the Hummingbird

Casey June Wolf

Well, I'm cheating on this. I'm the wolf, and that's only in name, not taxonomy. But the hummingbird was real, and this is our tale.

Last May I spent several weeks in the cabin of some friends in the mountains near Lillooet. One morning I woke quite late and focussed slowly on the Douglas fir boughs spreading out above the skylight. I grew conscious of the soft warmth of the big black and white cat that lay pressed against my cheek.

"Good morning!" I said.

"Mroww!" he replied, stretching.

"Time to feed Oriole and water the plants," I said. He said nothing, but hopped down to the floor as I got up.

A few minutes later we left the cabin, crossing the broken porch, stepping off the big stone stoop and passing between the lilac and the tall, white-flowering saskatoon.

We walked the long walk to the big house, where the horse and garden were, enacting much the same scene we did every day.

I travelled slowly, telling the cat about my dreams and musing over possible plans for the day. He moved more slowly still, sniffing every breeze, jumping when the trees jittered together high above our heads. Every few steps he'd quit walking and just sit down. Every few steps, therefore, I would stop, turn and call his name. "Se-le!"

Whenever I called he'd hop up and walk quickly towards me, tail high, sometimes catching up, sometimes even passing, sometimes lagging terribly far behind. He didn't want to stay at the cabin, he didn't want to hurry, and he didn't want to be carried. He walked exactly the way he wanted to walk. And I learned how to slow right down.

As we meandered towards the house, we passed clumps of dry grasses and spirea growing up the hill on our left and down the hill on our right. We passed fresh green snowberries, mock orange bushes, well-spaced

Douglas firs and low-growing Oregon grape. The cool, dry air was sweet and fascinating to our city noses.

After a while, I, and a little later the cat, came level with the corral, which lay a short distance downslope. There was the horse — Oriole — black and white like Sele. Her ears were forward in an alert expression, and she snorted and complained at the lateness of her hay. The cat stopped dead, stared, ready to run. I called, and slowly, slowly, he moved on and we made our way to the house.

Oriole kept muttering, Sele found a good-smelling tarp to rub on, and I set off for the outhouse. But when I popped inside, a terrible flurry erupted: a tiny bird hurled himself at the window again and again in an effort to get away.

I popped right back out, peering in the window at the little reddish-brown bird, noticing the green on his head and the black on his chin, and wondered what to do.

I held a hand to the window, thinking he might fly away from it and out the open doorway. But he only flew up more vigorously and banged against the glass again and again. I backed quickly out of sight.

Now, I had an important reason for going to that outhouse, so I took a chance and crept quietly, carefully back inside. The bird stayed calm, so I sat down and went about my business. As I did so, I studied him some more. Were my eyes deceiving me, or did he seem a bit weak? How long had he been trapped in here? I got up, put myself in order and moved to his left, hoping to encourage him to fly to the right and out the door. He went right, to the end of the window, and stopped. I waved my hands to get him to fly again, but he just buzzed helplessly and fell down to the shelf. So I scooped him up and covered him, stepped out of the outhouse, raised my arms in a dramatic sweep and opened my hands to let him fly away.

Minuscule feet gripped my finger. The tiny red body heaved with great breaths. He glanced around, blinked and huddled. He made no move to fly.

For several minutes I stood there, arms upraised. Maybe he didn't go because he was exhausted. Maybe he'd used up all his energy trying to escape the outhouse. Maybe he hadn't eaten in a long time. Very tiny, very busy animals need lots of food to keep them on the go. If I just put him down, he might be too tired to eat, and someone — I looked around nervously for the cat — might come by and eat *him*.

What to do?

I stared at the creature. He let his eyes close softly and rested in my hand. He isn't *dying*, is he? I asked myself. I couldn't tell.

But, oh, what a stunning bird he was! He was a lovely reddish-brown, with two darker, slender wings that seemed too small even for him. His tail was darker too, with white stripes, and fanned out like a ragged gown. The cap on his head was a brilliant green; it caught the light and threw it when he moved his head. He fit easily into my palm and weighed less than a fairy's breath.

I scrutinized him a while longer, searching my memory for facts about hummingbirds. I remembered that they dip their long beaks into tubular flowers, and that people attract them to feeders filled with sugar water by means of big red and yellow plastic flowers. I glanced around at the flower supply. Nothing even close to red. Could I take him in the house and feed him? I knew there was no sugar. Would honey do as well? I watched the pale tendril of his tongue as it slid out the end of his narrow bill. How could you forcefeed a mouth like that? You couldn't, I was sure. I would have to trick him into thinking he was being offered a flower.

Gently, I closed my hands, cupping him inside, and walked towards the house. I looked for a container to put him in, but they were all too big, too little, too dirty, too clean... I didn't want to scare him any more.

I walked him to the flowering plum, guessing it was the wrong flower. But it couldn't hurt to try. Nearly slipping on the steep hill, I held him to a white flower cluster; he only blinked and turned his head away.

I was reluctant to take him into the house in case he got loose and flew against one of the windows. I secured him gently in the fingers of one hand, turned the screechy doorknob and went inside.

I searched around the kitchen for something to make a fake plastic flower with. The noise made him struggle in my hand, so I emptied out the garlic basket, cleared off the cutting board and put him inside the makeshift cage. Light as the basket was, when he buzzed around for a moment in protest, he couldn't move it at all.

I found a red coffee lid and a bit of yellow Lego. These would have to suffice. I opened a tub of Golden Cariboo honey and put some in a cup, turned the only tap and let cold mountain water run into the cup, then stirred and stirred and stirred, determined to mix the firm honey into a runny broth. Finally I took it and the lid and the yellow bit out to the picnic table, and readied the plastic "flower." Then I brought out the upside-down basket and the cutting board with the hummingbird inside, closing the door behind me so he couldn't fly back in. As the door shut, the horse whinnied from the other side of the house. Poor Oriole. Her breakfast would have to wait a little more.

As I sat down I looked around for Sele. Still no sign of him. Good. A hint of guilt crept over me. He was probably feeling abandoned and nervous in this unfamiliar place.

I put the flower carefully under the basket.

No movement.

I pushed it closer to the hummingbird.

He didn't even look.

Desperate, I poked my finger into the mixture and slipped it under the basket and up to the bird's beak-tip. To my surprise, after a moment of stillness, the long tongue slipped out and trembled tentatively against the liquid on my finger. When he stopped drinking, I dipped the finger back into the mixture and held it to his mouth. Again he drank.

I frowned at the silly basket and lifted it away. He sat quietly, sipping at the honey water. When he blinked, I could see the black of his eyelid, with a tiny row of what looked like scales along its edge.

For several minutes we carried on, sitting in the sun, I dipping my finger into thicker and thinner mixtures of honey and water, seeing what he liked best, he drinking more and more greedily, his tongue flicking over and under my finger, sucking eagerly at the hanging drops of liquid. When he faced me, the orange-red feathers of his throat and breast blazed so brightly they were almost gold.

As he drank, the huddled, tired hummingbird changed ever so slowly into an alert, bold, energetic bird. At last, when I dipped my finger into the honey and brought it to his beak, he leapt up suddenly and flew to the flowering plum. I was so surprised I jumped, and for a moment was sorry to see him go, but as suddenly as he had flown I realized with delight that I had done what I wanted to do. A happy tear sprang up, and as I wiped it away, the hummingbird disappeared.

After a minute I got up, drank the rest of the honey-water and put the things back in the kitchen. I washed the plastic, put the garlic away, left the cutting board where it belonged. I went outside and called until I found the black and white cat, then went to the corral and fed the black and white horse. I lifted the lids on the cold frames and got out the hose and watered the potted plants. Then I sat with the cat on the warm ground and looked out at the little orchard. Sele was purring and rubbing beside me, none the worse for being left alone for half an hour.

The horse chewed happily behind the corral fence. I looked contentedly out at the orchard. I thought of the hummingbird, happy he was free, sad I wouldn't see him again. At that moment, a little red bird swooped from the Douglas firs across the yard and dove in a deep arc through the young fruit trees. Then he flew straight back, making a faint chittering call as he went. Instantly he turned and did it again, and then instantly again. I smiled. I got up, took the hose and watered the little apple trees and the drooping columbines. As I did so I heard again and again the thrum of his tiny wings.

I called the cat and walked out of the yard with him, past the munching horse, past the tarp, up the long road back to the cabin. And when I had my own late, late breakfast, I put a thick layer of Golden Cariboo honey on a piece of bread, in honour of my little friend.

Fox Dance
Colin Lamont

We loaded our rifles into Mark's old pickup before sunrise. As we drove slowly out of the yard, I could see a few fading stars reflected in the black-ice sky. The truck's headlights swept through cold northern shadows and I felt a shiver of anticipation. It was 1974. I was nineteen years old, and itching to get out into the bush for my first moose kill. My friend Mark and I had driven up from the Fraser Valley to Prince George and were staying with his sister and her husband. We had three full days to bag a bull moose, and we didn't plan on wasting even one hour.

Neither of us spoke as we blinked the sleep out of our eyes on that October morning. To be honest, I was also nervous about going hunting with my friend: he was, even for a country boy, gun crazy. His truck's rifle rack was loaded with a scoped .308, a double-barrelled 12-gauge shotgun, a single-barrel 16-gauge shotgun and a .22 rifle, plus my own .303 rifle. Mark was just a tad hyper by nature. Any cow, horse or hunter, including myself, that moved through the bush near him could end up well ventilated.

In spite of my own testosterone-driven urge to pack a rifle and sniff at wild-game spore, I was also nervous because I'd never killed an animal before. I'd grown up target shooting at a rod and gun club, but I wondered now what it would feel like to sight in on — with intent to kill — a living, breathing animal. To squeeze the trigger, hear the crack of the rifle and watch a heavy-antlered moose stagger on those ridiculously long legs, bellowing in pain, and then sink to its knees with blood soaking through its glossy, dark hide. I told myself that the moose wouldn't actually know what had hit it, that it would just topple over, dead. I argued with myself that the meat wouldn't be wasted; Mark and I and his sister's family would eat many a meal from it. I reminded myself that everyone shot deer and moose around Prince George. Hell, this was practically pioneer country; some families depended on putting a moose in the freezer for winter meat. I had certainly eaten wild venison before, but I was used to seeing it on my plate after the kill, when the animal had been gutted, butchered and wrapped neatly in heavy brown paper.

I even fantasized about stalking a wily bull that suddenly turned on us and charged, huge pug-ugly head lowered, fourteen hundred pounds of moose meat and a full rack barrelling straight at us. Mark would stumble as he took a shot — and miss. I'd calmly get the moose in my cross hairs and take it down with one clean shot. A clear case of self-defence.

We both relaxed as the pickup's cab warmed up from the heater, and we drank steaming coffee from a thermos. "Just remember to shoot for the neck area, not the head. That's your trophy," Mark said loudly, breaking the silence. He was a few years older than me and never stopped trying to impress me in his role as veteran hunter. "Don't spoil the meat by hitting it, just go for the neck," he repeated. I had my suspicions that he had never shot an animal larger than a pigeon or a squirrel. He would have stuffed a deer or moose head and mounted it on his truck.

A weak sun lit the pale-blue morning; dense forests of balsam, pine and spruce took shape on both sides of the almost empty highway. "Herds of moose could hide out there, but we have the map, so all we have to do is get 'em in our sights and knock 'em down," Mark said happily, taking one hand off the wheel to swing an imaginary rifle in front of my face.

I winced, then glanced down at our map on the front seat. It was not exactly the Michelin Guide to four-star moose-hunting. A few nights ago, we'd been whooping it up at the North Wood Inn, sitting at a table with Mark's sister, her husband and their logger buddies. Decked out in his new fluorescent orange hunting vest and cap, my friend started bragging. "I come up here to bag a moose every year, just to help out my sister, otherwise I wouldn't bother. After you hunt a few moose, there's no challenge," he said in a loud drawl. Most of the loggers just snorted and ignored him. After a few more beers, a logger called Cowboy conned Mark into buying two rounds, twenty-four beer, for our table. In return, Cowboy drew a hunting map on a napkin smeared with cheeseburger grease. "This map is guaranteed to take you close enough to smell the butt end of a humungous bull. I seen this moose personally and I know right where he hangs out," Cowboy swore to Mark.

Now, as we bumped down a logging road that had gone from wide gravel to narrow dirt track, I wondered where the napkin would take us. I had no faith in it or Cowboy. But it didn't really matter to me. I figured we were upping our chances of a kill the farther out in the sticks we went. The dirt tracks we were following kept squeezing in on us until tree branches slapped against the truck's doors; the track was getting muddier by the minute and I could feel the pickup's rear end start to sway from side to side. "Maybe we should back up and turn around," I finally suggested. Mark looked scornfully at me. "This is a highway compared to some roads I've driven on in the Yukon," he said flatly. Then he steered around a sharp bend and hit the binders.

A rusty metal gate, bent like a beer pretzel, blocked our path. It had recently served as a barrier across the dirt track and looked like the hit-and-run victim of a raging four-wheel driver.

On the other side of the gate was a small, abandoned garbage dump. From the look of things, it had probably been used by a gyppo logging company that had cut the best timber and left the worst junk behind. Dented oil cans, an old cookhouse stove, the twisted chassis of an ancient crummy, rusted logging cables and flattened food cans were all heaped together in mouldy piles. We surprised a few crows and ravens picking through the garbage, the first wildlife I'd seen that day. When they took flight, flapping and squawking, we saw our moose.

At least, we saw his remains: a stiff, black headless hide covered in dried blood, along with its front and back legs hacked off at about the knees, hooves still attached. Cowboy was right. Judging by the skin, it had been a huge bull, and we certainly could have walked up and smelled it if we had wanted to. Mark stared hard at the hide, blinking behind his glasses. "You must've read me the map wrong," he said finally. The sight of the dead moose tossed on the scrap heap had left me feeling tight inside and now I collapsed in nervous laughter, slapping my palm on the dash, tears rolling down my cheeks and lungs gasping for air. Mark just glared at me. He didn't start to laugh until I had to get out and push when the pickup bogged down in the mud. We were both soaked in sweat and coated in soggy clay by the time we got the truck back on dry pavement.

It was still only about ten o'clock and we had the whole day left to hunt. Mark was bitter about the map, but after we got back onto the highway we decided to try again, closer to town. We turned onto a paved side road lined with barbed-wire fences and empty cattle fields. The sun was now high enough to catch the crisp gold pattern of aspen leaves that brightened the countryside, and in the heated cab our muddy clothes began to dry out. I started to relax and enjoy the morning.

After about twenty minutes, the heat made me sleepy. I stared out the windshield, trying to concentrate on the quiet landscape. Then I glanced out the side window — straight at a silver fox dancing on its hind legs. It appeared suddenly, frolicking beside a mossy granite boulder, sleek black coat filled with sunlight and bushy, silver-tipped tail floating out behind as the fox pranced and hopped. Maybe it was a young fox kicking up its heels, or an adult dancing its mating steps. I had no idea why it was dancing, but I was mesmerized. I'd never seen a silver fox before, I didn't know foxes danced, and the dance seemed part of autumn, the colours, the snap in the air, the last burst of life before winter's sleep.

Mark slammed the truck to a stop. "Gimme the .22 and crank down your window!" he shouted. If I had opened the window, I believe he would have tried to shoot, the barrel about three inches in front of my face. Instead, while he shouted for blood, I flashed back to the moose hide in the dump.

"Quick, gimme the gun!" Mark roared again, and reached for the .22. I beat him to the draw and grabbed the barrel with both hands. "Just slide it to me," he shouted excitedly. I kept the .22 firmly in the rifle rack. "What the hell are you doin'? It'll get away," he said, groaning.

"You're not shooting from inside the goddamn cab, Mark. You'll hit me!" I shouted.

The truth was that when the sun had stroked the dancing fox, and I'd pictured the dead moose, the fox had killed the hunter in me before I fired a single shot.

Mark cooled down as the fox bounded away. We parked and hiked through the bush, but I'd had enough for the day. When my friend ran off to chase a grouse, I sat down. I listened to the distant ping of his .22 and I thought about dancing foxes. I sat there and I watched the leaves fall, twirling in the cold breeze that carried them down beside me.

The Souls of Animals

Lorna Crozier

"Having no souls, they have come,
Anyway, beyond their knowing."

— JAMES DICKEY, "The Heaven of Animals"

If animals have no souls
it's because they do not need them.
There is something forever about their time
on earth, whether they move on wing, paw or hoof,
or slide with huge, cold bodies
across the blue-green worlds.

Wherever they dwell, their gaze
when they look at you
comes from a great height —
the yellow of hawk and panther eye —
or so close up
they've slipped under the leaves
of your eyelids and stare from the inside out.

In books of the dead the human soul
becomes bird or butterfly
or soft-pawed, graceful thing.
Grant animals a soul: might it not leave
their bodies in the shape of ours?
Assume the best of us, the high forehead,
the shapely arms, the exactitude of
thumb on index finger.

That's what those bright ones are,
those people we glimpse with a glow about them,
an ecstacy. The souls of animals
crossing from one country to another,
pausing for a moment among us
only to rise in glory,
beasts again.

About the Authors

VIDYUT AKLUJKAR *is a poet, writer, lecturer and researcher with four books to her credit. She lives in Richmond with her husband, two children and two cats.*

DENISE ANDERSON, *an occasional freelance writer, lives in Vancouver with her rabbit, who thinks he's a dog.*

JANCIS M. ANDREWS *of West Vancouver, author of* Rapunzel, Rapunzel, Let Down Your Hair, *feels at one with the bird, insect, fish and animal kingdoms.*

SHARON ARUNDEL *is an aspiring writer living on the Sunshine Coast. She resides with two dogs, four cats and a friendly rat.*

CAROL BOSIER *is a writer/llama owner who lives in the Fraser Valley. Animals have taught her simplicity in dialogues with God, others and her inner self.*

MARY ELLEN BRADSHAW *is a freelance writer, Tai Chi instructor, wife and mother who lives in West Vancouver surrounded by beloved critters, both domestic and wild.*

BRIAN BRETT *is the author of several books of fiction and poetry, including* Tanganyika *and* Poems: New and Selected. *He currently lives with his family on Salt Spring Island.*

ANDREW BRYANT *is an independent conservation biologist. In addition to marmots, he is currently studying burrowing owls, forest songbirds and salamanders.*

PHIL BUTTERFIELD *teaches in 100 Mile House and lives in Bridge Lake with his wife and their two dogs, Baron and Daisy, as well as many migratory birds of all species.*

NEALL CALVERT, *an editor/writer/photographer/counsellor, lives near Pacific Spirit Regional Park in Vancouver. He believes animals make an inestimable, often unrecognized contribution to humans.*

MICHELE CARTER *is a Vancouver-born writer with a Master's degree in English. From birth to age ten, her best friend was Finnegan, a gentle, loving Irish water spaniel.*

NORMA CHARLES, *a teacher-librarian and writer of children's books, shares a rambling house in Vancouver with two old cats and various friends and children.*

LORNA CROZIER'S Inventing the Hawk *received the Governor General's Award for Poetry, the Canadian Authors' Association Award and the Pat Lowther Award. Her latest book is* Everything Arrives at the Light.

GLORIA DANYLUK *is a flight instructor working in Vernon. In her twenty years of aviation she has encountered many unusual animals — and people!*

WILLIAM DEVERELL *is the author of eight novels and one nonfiction book and is creator of the TV series* Street Legal. *He lives on North Pender Island with his wife, Tekla, and their cat, Martha.*

DON DICKINSON, *Lillooet author of three fiction books —* Fighting the Upstream, Blue Husbands *and* The Crew *— cannot live in a household without animals.*

SANDY FRANCES DUNCAN *lives on Gabriola Island. She has published seven novels for children and adults, and is looking for a bumper sticker: I brake for frogs.*

TONY EBERTS, *his wife, Dorothy, and two dogs inhabit five overgrown acres near Aldergrove. A retired newspaperman, he's now a birder and angler who freelances on environmental issues.*

RICK FAVELLE *has worked with the S.P.C.A. since 1982 and found it to be extremely rewarding. He has hundreds more rescue stories he could tell.*

MARY C. FOSTER *is an Abbotsford senior. During WWII she did farm work in England as a volunteer member of the Women's Land Army, and from 1969-71 she was kennel manager of the S.P.C.A. in Winnipeg.*

LOLADAWN FRIAS *is presently incarcerated at the Burnaby Correctional Centre for Women. Luke is content with his new family, but he occasionally visits his friends in prison.*

KIT GIFFORD *has lived in the Queen Charlottes for twenty-seven years. She writes, weaves, knits, gardens, reads and enjoys her cats, parrot and all wild creatures.*

TIM GILLARD *is a professional photographer based in Victoria. He lived in Fort St. John for eighteen years and misses the North very much.*

LEONA GOM *is a writer from White Rock. Having lived for twenty years on a homestead, she knows we owe a great debt to animals.*

REENE GRANLIN, *a freelance writer from Telkwa, enjoys observing, researching and writing about wildlife.*

MARIAM HABIB *was born in Africa and has written about many animals — felines, canines, bovines and humans. She lives in Vancouver.*

ROBERT HARLOW *is the author of seven published novels. He lives on a Gulf Island with writer Sally Ireland and a cat named Oliver J. Manx.*

KENNETH BRUCE HARRIS, *a member of the Kitwangak band of the Gitksan Nation, now lives in Vancouver. He holds the clan chief's title, 'Simoiqet Hagbegwatxw, which he inherited from his uncle.*

MONICA M. HILBORN *is a chemical engineer. She and her husband live in Delta with two cats and a dog. Her hobbies are horses, horses and horses.*

Singer/composer JUDY HILL *is a banker and future travel agent who lives in Chilliwack with her husband, Brad, and their three-legged golden retriever, Kate.*

CARRIE R. JEWELL *is a Touch for Health practitioner in Salmon Arm. She loves being with animals because they are so smart, cute and amusing and create a peacefulness in her soul.*

JANICE JOHNSON *shares a little peek-a-boo sun farm in Powell River with eighteen chickens, nine neutered/spayed wild cats and a very understanding husband.*

MICHAEL DAVID JOHNSON *was born on January 27, 1982, in Richmond. He loves ice hockey, baseball and basketball and likes to listen to music.*

DEANNA KAWATSKI *writes a regular column for* Mother Earth News *magazine. Her story is excerpted from her book* Wilderness Mother. *She prefers wild animals.*

D. C. KILPATRICK, *a lifetime resident of Vancouver, is co-owner of Sea Winds Florist. He and his wife live with Chase, a golden retriever, and O'Reilly, a Burmese kitten.*

COLIN LAMONT *is a Vancouver writer who shoots animals only with a camera. His writing has appeared in Canadian newspapers, magazines and books.*

GWEN LARIVIERE *is a Vancouver Island writer who presently lives in Sooke. She feels that the joy and wonder animals bring us is magnified tenfold by their incorrupt spirit.*

CATHERINE LEBREDT *and her husband, Mike, raised their daughter, April, now twelve, amongst the wildlife in Clayoquot Sound. Catherine Lebredt died in April 1995.*

AL LONGAIR, *a confirmed humaniac, attended the Western College of Veterinary Medicine at the University of Saskatchewan. He currently lives and works in the Cowichan Valley.*

EVE MACLEAN *was born and raised on an Ontario farm. In northern B.C., where she lived from 1911 until her death in 1984, she pursued her talents in music and writing.*

VICTORIA MILES *is a freelance writer with a background in communications and environmental education. She is the author of four children's picture books featuring British Columbia wildlife.*

HAZEL I. MILLER *lives in Nelson. She remembers her childhood pets and deplores the cruelty and indignities to which circus and rodeo animals are subjected.*

GWENDOLINE S. MOWATT, *now a widow, has cared for animals her whole life, especially injured animals, nursing many of them back to health.*

GEORGE N. MURRAY *is an electrical contractor who lives aboard his sailboat. A fanatical outdoorsman, he is very interested in animal behaviour.*

BRIAN D. OBERQUELL, *a freelance SPFX technician, lives in Port Moody with Mary, his wife, and Toby, his chocolate Rex buck.*

LORETTA OLUND *lives in Surrey. She has owned and worked with various animals in her life, including birds, reptiles and small and large mammals.*

MARILYN PITERS, *employed by the Ministry of Health, shares her home with lawyer husband Ron, their two children and a wide assortment of animals.*

HOLLY BARBER PUGSLEY *and her husband, Den, have lived around Williams Lake since 1981. They are janitors. Holding the trust of an animal is most important to her.*

ELAINE REGIER, *a teacher, wife and mother of four children, lives on a hobby farm in Aldergrove. Her family enjoys caring for various farm animals.*

SAM RODDAN, *a long-time contributor to the* Vancouver Sun, *lives at Crescent Beach. He loves dogs, goats and all forms of life.*

SANDY SHREVE *lives in Vancouver and is communications coordinator for the Legal Services Society. The events in "Whale Watching" occurred on Pender Island in 1991.*

ELIZABETH THUNSTROM *lives in Coquitlam and works as a wildlife rehabilitator at Wildlife Rescue. She has always been fascinated by animals and the natural environment.*

HERMINA A. VAN GAALEN, *a zooarchaeologist living in Coquitlam, has had all sorts of animals gracing most of her life. Each pet was unique, loved and needed.*

JACQUELINE WARD *is a teacher/farmer from Qualicum Beach. Five dogs and numerous farm animals share her life, usually living a more pampered existence than she does.*

STEVEN WASYLIK *currently lives near Nelson. He has been a conservation officer for ten years. He obtained his dog, Max, from the Surrey S.P.C.A. in 1986.*

Pender Harbour resident HOWARD WHITE, *the founder of Harbour Publishing, is the editor of* Raincoast Chronicles *and the author of seven books, including the Stephen Leacock Award–winning* Writing in the Rain.

CASEY JUNE WOLF *lives in Vancouver with three ex-stray cats and her step-fish. She has volunteered for the Northwest Wildlife Preservation Society for six years.*

LINDA WOOD *lives in New Westminster, where she works with International Education. For her, concern for animals is a way of life, not just a job or a membership.*

SANDRA BETTE YATES, *a lactation consultant/breast-feeding counsellor living in North Vancouver, feels that nurturing babies, whether human or animal, is the most important work there is.*

Acknowledgements

This book came about through the individual and collective efforts of many people who care about animals. Thank-you first of all to the more than six hundred writers who submitted their work. Special thanks are due to the published authors who responded so generously with donated work. Those whose entries are not included in *How I Learned to Speak Dog and Other Animal Stories* should take consolation from the fact that a great deal of excellent material had to be omitted for lack of space. Thanks too to Rose Cowles, the book's designer and cover illustrator, who donated the appealing text illustrations.

Thanks to Dayle Crawferd of Surrey, B.C., who creates and sells handmade greeting cards to support humane education. Her donations provided the seed money to initiate the project.

One of our concerns was that the book be provincewide in scope. For their assistance in spreading the word, thank-you to Cecilia Walters and the crew on CBC Radio's *Almanac*, to guest storyteller Nicola Cavendish and to the many community newspapers and radio stations that invited their readers and listeners to participate. At the *Vancouver Sun*, which printed the call for stories and a selection of the best entries, thank-you to Ian Haysom, Scott Honeyman, Karenn Krangle and Nicholas Read.

An enormous and heartfelt thank-you goes to the members of the volunteer editorial committee — Alma Lee, Elizabeth MacLean, Maureen Medved, Victoria Miles, Sherry Pettigrew, Nicholas Read, Cat Simril, Eileen Stubbe, Judith McBride, Darlene Tavares, Jody Doll and Randall Doll. Members of this committee met many times over the past year to design and monitor the project, to read and review all of the entries, and to create and maintain a database of submissions and authors with the help of Lil Russ. The committee includes several professional editors who devoted hours to polishing prose. And on behalf of both the committee and the B.C. S.P.C.A., thank-you to Vicki Gabereau, an early champion of the book and an inspiration to storytellers everywhere.

It is a pleasure to acknowledge the support of the B.C. S.P.C.A. board, its Committee of Management and the B.C. S.P.C.A. Centennial Committee; the staff of the B.C. S.P.C.A. provincial office; the board and staff of the B.C. Humane Education Society; and the boards, staff and volunteers of the B.C. S.P.C.A.'s thirty-three branches. This book honours 100 years of the B.C. S.P.C.A.'s unceasing dedication to animal welfare.

Part of the mandate of the B.C. S.P.C.A. Centennial has been to build cooperative relationships with other animal welfare organizations. While there are certainly times when, as organizations, we may disagree on tactics, we are fortunate in the British Columbia animal welfare movement to share an overriding sense of the greater good for which we all strive. Thank-you then to the following organizations and their members who participated in the creation of the book: B.C. Pets & Friends; B.C. Veterinary Medical Association; Critter Care Wildlife Society; Federation of B.C. Naturalists; Fur-Bearers Association; Greater Vancouver Urban Wildlife Committee; Meow-Aid; Mercy Volunteers for Animals; Northwest Wildlife Preservation Society; Vancouver Humane Society; and Wildlife Rescue Association.

Two months before this book was due at the publisher's, I suffered a broken back in a skiing accident. It thus fell to two people to coordinate the myriad of tasks involved in getting the manuscript completed on time. For their cheerful dedication and willingness to shoulder an additional workload, special thanks are due to my assistant, Darlene Tavares, and to our editor at Douglas & McIntyre, Barbara Pulling. Thanks also to Janice Bearg, Douglas & McIntyre's general manager, and to publisher Scott McIntyre.

And thank-you, finally, to the animals.

Stephen Huddart